CAMBRIDGE LIBRARY COLLECTION

Books of enduring scholarly value

British and Irish History, Nineteenth Century

This series comprises contemporary or near-contemporary accounts of the political, economic and social history of the British Isles during the nineteenth century. It includes material on international diplomacy and trade, labour relations and the women's movement, developments in education and social welfare, religious emancipation, the justice system, and special events including the Great Exhibition of 1851.

Hints on Self-Help

A determined campaigner for women's rights, Jessie Boucherett (1825–1905) helped to draft Britain's first female suffrage petition in 1866 and founded the *Englishwoman's Review* in the same year. Originally published in 1863 and reissued here in its 1866 printing, the present work is her call to arms for young women of all classes to pursue their independence through education and employment. Emphasising the risk of trusting in men to provide for women, she urges her readers to support themselves, first through education and then through remunerative work. She includes examples of the various trades open to women and examines the cases of women who have not only succeeded but excelled in their occupations. The appendices give details of institutions where women could receive training. Reflecting and refining the Victorian concern with self-improvement, this work remains relevant to social historians and readers interested in the women's movement.

T0382028

Cambridge University Press has long been a pioneer in the reissuing of out-of-print titles from its own backlist, producing digital reprints of books that are still sought after by scholars and students but could not be reprinted economically using traditional technology. The Cambridge Library Collection extends this activity to a wider range of books which are still of importance to researchers and professionals, either for the source material they contain, or as landmarks in the history of their academic discipline.

Drawing from the world-renowned collections in the Cambridge University Library and other partner libraries, and guided by the advice of experts in each subject area, Cambridge University Press is using state-of-the-art scanning machines in its own Printing House to capture the content of each book selected for inclusion. The files are processed to give a consistently clear, crisp image, and the books finished to the high quality standard for which the Press is recognised around the world. The latest print-on-demand technology ensures that the books will remain available indefinitely, and that orders for single or multiple copies can quickly be supplied.

The Cambridge Library Collection brings back to life books of enduring scholarly value (including out-of-copyright works originally issued by other publishers) across a wide range of disciplines in the humanities and social sciences and in science and technology.

Hints on Self-Help

A Book for Young Women

JESSIE BOUCHERETT

CAMBRIDGE
UNIVERSITY PRESS

CAMBRIDGE
UNIVERSITY PRESS

University Printing House, Cambridge, CB2 8BS, United Kingdom

Cambridge University Press is part of the University of Cambridge.
It furthers the University's mission by disseminating knowledge in the pursuit of
education, learning and research at the highest international levels of excellence.

www.cambridge.org
Information on this title: www.cambridge.org/9781108067805

This edition first published 1866
This digitally printed version 2014

ISBN 978-1-108-06780-5 Paperback

HINTS ON SELF-HELP.

HINTS ON SELF-HELP;

A

BOOK FOR YOUNG WOMEN.

BY

JESSIE BOUCHERETT.

"I would wish to impress on young people who are beginning life, as I did, dependent on their own exertions, the absolute need of concentrated industry; a definite purpose, and, above all conduct dictated by common sense."— LADY MORGAN.

LONDON:

JARROLD AND SONS, 12, PATERNOSTER ROW.

1866.

Dedicated

TO THE

PRESIDENT, VICE-PRESIDENTS, AND COMMITTEE

OF THE

Society for Promoting the Employment of Women.

PRESIDENT.
RIGHT HON. THE EARL OF SHAFTESBURY.

VICE-PRESIDENTS.
RIGHT REV. THE LORD BISHOP OF LONDON.
RIGHT REV. THE LORD BISHOP OF OXFORD.
RIGHT HON. W. E. GLADSTONE, M.P.
VICE-CHANCELLOR SIR WILLIAM PAGE WOOD.

COMMITTEE.

E. Akroyd, Esq.
Mrs. Aldridge.
Edwin Arnold, Esq.
*Mrs. Bayne.
Miss Jessie Boucherett.
Stephen Cave, Esq. M.P.
*W. Strickland Cookson, Esq.
*Miss Isa Craig.
*Miss Crowe.
The Lady Elizabeth Cust.
Mrs. Dalrymple.
*Miss Davies.
The Lady Alice Des Voeux.
Sir F. Goldsmid, Bart., M.P.
*Hon. Victoria Grosvenor.

Mrs. Richard Hoare.
Lord Houghton.
Miss James.
*Hon. Mrs. Locke King.
Hon. Arthur Kinnaird, M.P.
*Mrs. Lankester.
*Miss Lawrence.
Rev. C. Mackenzie, M.A.
Mrs. Wykeham Martin.
Rev. Francis Pigou, M.A.
Hon. Mrs. H Ponsonby.
*W. Bayne Ranken, Esq.
Hon. W. Spring Rice.
Mrs. P. A. Taylor.

Also to those who kindly afforded assistance to the Society in its early days, but who, from various causes, are no longer on the Committee.

INTRODUCTION.

THE object of this little work is to convey instruction
to young women on the Conditions of Industrial Success,
in an easy and popular manner, and to illustrate the
subject by examples of successful industry in persons of
their own sex.

It is a subject on which women generally have little
knowledge, and the ill effects of this ignorance are
shown in the large number of those who, when compelled
to try to maintain themselves, fail in the attempt.

These failures are not confined to one class only, but
extend to all, from the gentlewoman, who, by the misfortunes of her family, is unexpectedly thrown on her
own exertions for support, to the labourer's daughter,
who has been brought up in the knowledge that she
would have to earn her bread by manual labour.

To begin with the failures of the highest class.

The Governesses' Benevolent Institution had, on the

31st of December, 1861, 102 annuitants on the charitable fund, 22 in the Asylum, and 142 applicants for
annuities.

The Corporation of the Sons of the Clergy has a long
list of aged single women, daughters of clergymen, dependent on it for support.

In London and elsewhere there are numerous charities to assist distressed gentlewomen—Homes for Poor
Ladies, half self-supporting, half kept up by subscrip-
tions ; and Repositories, where fancy work, executed by
the same class, may be purchased by the benevolent.
Yet, numerous as are these charities, they are still insufficient for the task before them, as the report of
every one which has come before me testifies ; for each
speaks, either of deserving cases left unaided from
want of funds, or else complains that the assistance
which can be afforded is inadequately small. In one
case it is stated that a poor lady-worker for a repository
actually died of want. Workhouse visitors tell us that
in the wards it is not unusual to find women who have
known "better days," and evidently belong to a higher
rank than ordinary paupers.

In the lower ranks, too, sad failures occur. The oft-
told tale of the shirt-maker,—

> "Sewing at once, with a double thread,
> A shroud as well as a shirt,"

has lost its force by repetition, yet is not less true or

less terrible now, than when Hood wrote his famous song.

That much of this misery arises in all classes from ignorance of the necessary conditions of industrial success is my belief, and the belief of others who have studied the subject.

One common cause of failure is the impression prevalent among both parents and daughters of every class, that unskilled female industry is of value ; thus in no class are sufficient pains taken to prepare girls for their future avocations, and not until too late is it understood that a willing heart is of small avail in earning a livelihood, if united to unexercised brains and unskilful hands.

It is my object to combat this and other false notions ; to set forth under what circumstances a woman may hope to succeed in supporting herself, and when she must necessarily fail ; what will conduce to her success, and what bring on a failure.

In the Appendix are given the addresses of several institutions, where girls and young women may be taught various useful employments, suitable to different ranks and degrees of education. From these addresses well-taught and specially-trained young women may also be obtained by those who require their services. I have given, too, some hints as to the description of persons required in the Colonies. It has been my object to write a useful yet readable book. If I have attained to any degree of success, I am bound to acknowledge that it is greatly owing to the assistance I have received from the perusal of Mr. Smiles' book for young men on "Self-Help," from which I have often quoted, and have taken many valuable ideas.

CONTENTS.

CHAPTER IV.

DUTY AND INDEPENDENCE.

CHAPTER V.

MONEY: HOW TO WASTE IT—HOW TO KEEP IT.

CHAPTER VI.

SELF-RESPECT.—EXAMPLE.—INFLUENCE.

CHAPTER VII.

BENEFIT SOCIETIES FOR WOMEN.

CHAPTER VIII.

HEAD-WORK AND HEART-WORK.

APPENDIX A.

APPENDIX B.

APPENDIX C.

APPENDIX D.

HINTS ON SELF-HELP.

CHAPTER I.

Benefits of Self-Help.

> Let us, then, be up and doing,
> With a heart for any fate,
> Still achieving, still pursuing,
> Learn to labour and to wait.—*Longfellow.*

THE ideas of many young women with regard to self-help seem to be much on a level with those of the farmer in the old fable of " The Lark and her Young." Indeed, the story is so much to the purpose, that I will relate it for the benefit of those readers who may not happen to be acquainted with it.

" Once upon a time, a lark made her nest in a hay-field, near a footpath. When her young were hatched she went out every day to fetch them food, directing them meanwhile to keep quiet, and listen to everything that was said by the passers-by, that they might find out when the grass was to be cut.

" One day, on her return, the young ones cried out,

with much excitement, ' O mother ! we must at once
leave our nest, the grass is to be cut directly, for the
farmer passed by this morning with his son, and said,
that as the grass was ready and the weather fine, he
should send out to call his friends and neighbours to
come and help him to make hay, and they are going to
begin to-morrow.' ' Do not fear, my children,' said the
old bird, ' there is no need for us to move yet, the grass
will not be cut to-morrow ;' and, accordingly, they
remained undisturbed.

" Some days afterwards, the young larks again called
out in a arm, ' O mother ! the time has now, indeed,
come when we must fly ; for the farmer has been again,
and said that as his friends and neighbours had failed to
assist him, he should now send to his relations and call
on them to help him to cut the grass to-morrow.'
' There is no danger yet,' replied the mother. A few
more days passed, and again the young birds told their
mother, ' The farmer has been here, and says that as
both friends and relations have failed him, he will set
about cutting the grass himself to-morrow morning.'
' Now, indeed,' said the old hen, ' we must remove ; as
long as he trusted to others to help him there was little
chance of the hay being made, but now that he talks of
helping himself there is the greatest danger.' Accordingly they at once removed into another field, and
next morning the grass was cut; but meanwhile the
weather had changed, the sky was overcast, and presently
a heavy rain came on, which spoiled the hay."

The fate which overtook the farmer is very apt to
befall those young women, also, who trust that some one

else will provide for them: sometimes they hope that their friends and relations will leave them a comfortable income; sometimes that a good marriage will present itself, and save them the trouble of working for themselves; and so, instead of being "up and doing," they sit at home and wait, and time passes by, and too often it happens that their friends and relatives do nothing, and the good marriage does not present itself, or, if it does, is not agreeable to their taste, and is rejected, and so at last, when their parents die, they find themselves unprovided for; meanwhile youth, the best working time, has passed away, and when, at last, they do begin to try to earn their bread, they find themselves unable to do it, their hay is spoilt, and their life, which began so cheerfully, ends in sadness and sorrow, and in vain regrets for the lost opportunity. An Arab proverb says, "A sped arrow, a spoken word, and a lost opportunity, can never be recalled;" and the truth of this they find to their cost.

Yet, to those who have health and strength, the necessity of working is no great misfortune; for they who engage in a life of action are generally happier than they who are condemned to idleness.

The Marquis of Spinola asking Sir Horace Vere what his brother died of, Sir Horace replied, "He died, sir, of having nothing to do." "Alas," said Spinola, "that is enough to kill any of us generals." It is not, however, generals only who suffer from this complaint, as it is common enough for people of all sorts to fall into low spirits and bad health if they have no active occupation.

But to obtain success,—and by success I mean the power to earn an independent livelihood in youth, and a provision against old age,—willingness to work is not the only quality necessary; several other qualifications are wanted, and of these thoroughness and accuracy are the chief.   The value of knowledge consists not in its quantity, but in the uses to which it may be applied. The phrase in common use as to the "spread of knowledge" at this day is no doubt correct; but it is spread in such thin layers as to be of little practical use, and the number of those is rapidly increasing who know a little of everything and nothing well.

Such persons have not inaptly been likened to a certain sort of pocket knife which some people carry about with them, and which in addition to a common knife, contains a file, a chisel, a saw, a gimlet, a screw-driver, and a pair of scissors, but all so diminutive that the moment they are needed for use they are found useless.*   This universal superficial knowledge and special ignorance is commoner among women than men, in consequence of the inferiority of the education they receive; for women are generally taught a smattering of several sciences and accomplishments, but nothing is really mastered; and this is doubly injurious, because they not only remain ignorant of what would have proved useful to them in future life, but they acquire a *habit* of inaccurate and ineffective working.   Young women should, therefore, be on their guard against this propensity, which, natural to all, has been in them artificially

* This comparison and the anecdote about Spinola are taken from "Self-Help," by S. Smiles.

fostered and developed: they should endeavour, by careful self-training, to cure themselves of this defect.

One thing well understood, one art carried to perfection, is worth twenty pieces of imperfect knowledge. For instance, the tradesman's daughter, who writes well and is quick at accounts, will be more useful in her father's shop, or better able to get a situation elsewhere, than another who writes ill and does accounts wrong, but has some knowledge of French and a notion of painting in water-colours and playing on the pianoforte. Yet painting and music, when carried to excellence, are capital professions. Excellence can, however, only be attained by great study. Two or three hours a-day must be devoted to the practice of these arts for some years before much skill is attained, and really first-rate musicians and painters spend at least five hours a-day in playing and painting. Whoèver, therefore, wishes to excel in one of these pursuits, should devote herself to that only and leave the other alone, as no woman can have physical strength enough to enable her to study both effectively. If the object in learning is only amusement, a slight knowledge of· both may be obtained, enough probably to afford pleasure to the performer and her friends; but unless she possesses unusual abilities, the proficiency thus gained will never enable her to earn a shilling, except perhaps in teaching beginners. Besides accuracy and thoroughness, another qualification is necessary to success; indeed, without it, it is difficult to be accurate or thorough. The foundation of all excellence is the general power of reasoning, added to which must be the skill obtained by long practice in the particular branch to which we intend to apply ourselves.

Knowledge is one thing, the power of making use of it is another, and no knowledge can be said to be useful until its possessor can apply it to practical purposes, and to do this he or she must be able to reason. People with strong memories, but deficient in reason, may know multitudes of facts, which they will never be able to make of the least service to them. Cardinal Mezzofanti had a wonderful memory, and could speak fifty languages; but he never made the least use of his learning, and for any service he was to the world might just as well have been ignorant. Talleyrand, a witty and distinguished Frenchman, said of him, "He can speak fifty languages, but cannot say anything worth hearing in one of them." Reason is the master, memory the servant; a very useful servant if well directed, but otherwise of small utility. To give an illustration. A person may remember that the sun rises in the east and sets in the west, yet may not be able to guide himself in the least by this knowledge, nor even to tell in what direction he is travelling. Or, a woman may have learned everything in the arithmetic book about square root, yet be puzzled to find out how many yards of carpeting she wants for her parlour floor, or how many strips of paper for the walls. Thus, there may be knowledge without the capability of applying it. On this account, for the sake of rendering knowledge useful, the power of reasoning should be sedulously cultivated.

Self-reliance, when founded on self-knowledge, is another valuable quality, but when not so founded it partakes somewhat of the character of self-conceit, and is often mischievous. True self-knowledge can only be obtained by experience; it is, therefore, advisable to allow young people as much liberty of action as is consistent with prudence, that they may make attempts on a small scale, achieve little successes, and sustain little defeats, by which they will learn the strong and weak points of their own characters, and so prepare themselves for real life.

Want of confidence is, perhaps, a greater obstacle to improvement than is generally imagined. True modesty is quite compatible with a due estimate of one's own deserts, and does not demand the abnegation of all merit.

The celebrated divine, Dr. Butler, defines humility as thinking *truly* of one's self, putting a just estimate on one's own powers, not in thinking less well of one's self than one really deserves. A just estimate of one's own merit cannot be attained without trial; and thus it is that people who do nothing often have such an unduly high opinion of themselves; never having tried to do anything they have never failed, and, therefore, are apt to despise others who have tried and failed, though, perhaps, if these boastful persons were to try, they would make a still greater failure.

Thus, effort and action produce a just estimate of our powers: those who are inclined to think too well of themselves find their mistake by experience, while those who think too poorly of their merits are agreeably surprised by success in their undertaking. On this account, if on no other, a life of action is more improving than a life of idleness. There are, doubtless,

many conceited young women who deceive themselves
by thinking too highly of their abilities; yet more, I
believe, fail from want of confidence in themselves and
faith in their own powers.

It has been observed by Mr. Smiles that half the
failures in life arise from stopping one's horse when
about to jump; and Dr. Johnson was accustomed to
attribute all his success to confidence in his own
powers. It is often the case that the reason why so
little is done is that so little is attempted. We do not
succeed simply because we are too much depressed to
try. One step forward would help us, but that one
step we do not take. The right plan is, to do our duty
and try our best, leaving the result with God. If we
fail, we fail; but it is more honourable to try, and fail,
than never to have tried at all: and even from a failure
we may learn something which may enable us to succeed
another time.

CHAPTER II.

Perseverance.—Business Habits.

> By patient toil great deeds are done;
> By waiting long the victory's won;
> Wisdom is learn'd by errors past,
> And failure brings success at last.

It is a great point to begin well, for the proverb "Well begun is half done" is true. Its truth lies in this, the person who is cheered by a little success at first is encouraged to persevere. The success is, perhaps, worth but little in itself, but its moral effect in preventing despondency is worth much. The great highway of human welfare lies along the old road of steadfast well-doing, and, if all other circumstances are equal, they who are the most persistent and work in the truest spirit will invariably be the most successful.

"Fortune has been blamed for her blindness, but she is not as blind as men are. Those who look into practical life will find that fortune is usually on the side of the industrious, as the winds and waves are on the side of the best navigators.

"Success treads on the heels of every right effort;

and though it is possible to over-estimate the merit of
success to the extent of almost deifying it, as is sometimes done, still, in any worthy pursuit it is creditable
to succeed.   Nor are the qualities necessary to win
success at all extraordinary; they may, for the most
part, be summed up in these two—Common Sense and
Perseverance.

"Genius belongs to few, and is not necessary in every-
day life, though even genius does not despise the exercise
of these common qualities.   The very greatest men have
been among the least believers in the power of genius,
and have shown themselves as wise and persevering as
successful men of a common sort.   Some have even
defined genius to be common sense intensified.   A distinguished teacher and president of a college spoke of it
as 'the power of making efforts.'   Buffon, the great
naturalist, said of genius, 'It is patience.'" *

Rosa Bonheur is a remarkable instance of the success
attendant on genius joined to perseverance and firmness
of character.   She was born in 1822, the daughter of a
poor Parisian drawing-master, and during her early years
displayed no particular genius, though an old friend
of her father's, with whom she was a favourite, used to
augur from her vigorous and resolute character that she
would, some day, turn out a remarkable woman.

When twelve years old, she was apprenticed to a
dressmaker, a profession that was utterly distasteful to
her, as her chief pleasure was wandering about in the
open air.   At last, distress of mind and confinement

* From "Smiles' Self-Help."

made her ill; her father, therefore, broke off the arrangement, and took her home. Soon afterwards, she was
sent to school, where, however, she showed aptitude for
nothing but drawing.

On leaving school, she was left a good deal to herself,
and employed her time in modelling figures of animals in
her father's studio, and in copying his paintings. It
occurred to her, that by this means she might be able,
some day, to support herself, perhaps attain to what had
always been her secret ambition, *to be something;* so she
worked hard all day, and day after day. Her father,
amazed at her progress, and perceiving her talent, devoted himself seriously to her instruction, and after
taking her through a course of preparatory study, sent
her to the Louvre to copy the fine pictures there, as a
discipline for her eye, hand, and judgment.

It was remarked that she was the first to enter the
gallery in the morning, and the last to leave it in the
evening. "I have never seen an example of such application and such ardour for work," remarked the Director
of the Louvre, in speaking of her. At last, her copies
began to sell; she got but a small sum for each, but felt
it delightful to be able to relieve her father of some part
of her support, and she worked hard that she might make
more copies.

At this period she was only sixteen years old, so she
had wasted no time. One day, having made a study
of a goat, she was so pleased with her success, that she
determined to devote herself to painting animals. Too
poor to procure models, she went out daily on foot into
the country to sketch the sheep and cows.

With a bit of bread in her pocket, she used to start early in the morning, laden with her painting materials, and having found a subject to her mind, would seat herself on a bank or under a tree, and work till evening, coming home at nightfall, after a walk of many miles, browned by the sun and wind, or soaked with rain and covered with mud ; but rejoicing in the lessons the day had furnished.   Rosa Bonheur used also to go to the enclosures where the animals are kept previous to being sent to the slaughter-houses, overcoming alike her natural repugnance to such a vicinity and to placing herself in contact with the crowds of butchers and drovers who were standing about.   There, seated on a bundle of hay, she would sketch from morning till night ; but such was the respect her simple earnestness in art occasioned, that an uncivil word was never spoken to her. When at home, she kept a pet sheep on the leads, outside her attic window, that she might always have a model to copy from.   At last, this hard work was rewarded, for, in 1841, when nineteen years of age, she exhibited three paintings of animals which were much admired.   From this period, she exhibited in all the Paris exhibitions, and won several bronze and silver medals.   At last she won the gold medal, a great distinction, and, what was still more delightful, was able to relieve her father from all pecuniary embarrassments by the sale of her pictures.

In 1853, she exhibited her famous picture of the "Horse Market," the preparatory studies for which had occupied her during eighteen months. This picture sold for £1600, and has been resold for much more, and from

that time her reputation and fortune were made. She
is now very wealthy, and is recognized as the best
animal-painter of the day in Europe. Her success has
benefitted not herself only, but others of her own sex,
for, until lately, women were not admitted to study at
the Royal Academy in England, there being, probably,
an impression on the minds of the gentlemen who managed it, that it was useless to teach women, as they
could never excel. Rosa Bonheur's success dispelled
this notion, and not long ago, women were admitted as
pupils ; so, some years hence, we also may hope to have
a distinguished female artist among us. It is much to
the credit of French liberality, that they have for several
years admitted female artists to study at the Louvre
under the Director; had they not done so, Rosa
Bonheur, deprived of good instruction, might never
have become a great artist, and people would have continued to believe that women were incapable of painting
well. No amount of good teaching, however, could
have made her win her present position, unless she
had possessed courage and perseverance to surmount
obstacles to success, and diligence to study at every
opportunity.

Great success like this can only be attained by extraordinary talents ; but success enough to produce
happiness can usually be attained by simple means
and the exercise of ordinary abilities, if united to industry and perseverance, and, above all, to courage and
energy.

Miss B—— had a slight knowledge of wood-engraving,
by which she wished to earn her living. Some friends

undertook to pay the expense of her instruction and lodging in town; so she came up to study, and studied hard, getting up at five in the morning to practise. She had both perseverance in learning, and in doing the work, and energy, when she had learned, to go about and get orders, without which her previous labours would have been wasted; this is a point on which women often fail. They should always bear in mind that industry in learning is seldom of use, unless they have courage and energy to go from employer to employer, exhibiting specimens of their work, and soliciting orders; and this rule does not apply to wood-engraving only, but to many other arts and handicrafts.

Miss B——'s energy met its reward. She began to earn much earlier than usual, even with men, and has good prospects of success. She is now married, but as her work can be carried on at home, she fully intends to go on with it.*

Another young person, M—— N——, has shown even greater perseverance and courage. Early in life, her relatives wished her to set up a small day-school; but this she resisted, having no vocation for the employment, and, instead, persuaded a friend of hers at York to teach her hair-dressing and cutting, and something of the general trade; then she went up to town to get finishing lessons.

Having thus attained to a knowledge of her business,

---

* It is not at all desirable that married women should engage in work which takes them away from home. This is the rule; but, of course, there are exceptions.

she went about to country houses and villages canvassing
for orders, and succeeded in establishing a connection
sufficient for her own support. As she was skilful in
her work, the business increased, till it became too
large for herself alone, and she took both her sisters
into it. All three earn a good livelihood, and help to
support their grandmother into the bargain. M——
N—— comes up to town every year to study any
changes that may have taken place in the fashion of
hair-dressing, and to renew her stock in trade.

When going her rounds in the country, she wears a
large clean white apron, with pockets, and long white
cuffs up to the elbow, beneath her cloak. She goes
out in the evening to dress ladies' hair for country
balls, and will go ten or twelve miles if she hopes to
find a good new opening; and besides this, she makes
circuits through the country to little towns and villages,
giving notice that she is coming, that she may serve
her scattered customers. Thus, by energy and industry, this meritorious woman has established herself
and sisters in a good profitable business, and set an
example which may be imitated with advantage. No
extraordinary ability was required to do this, only such
talents as hundreds of other women possess, united to
a love of independence, and a spirit of enterprize and
industry.

Nor ought persons unendowed with remarkable capacity to rest content in dependence on the kindness
of others for support. Every one ought to be able to
say, as a famous German writer did, "I have made as

much out of myself as can be made out of the stuff, and
no man should require more." *

Society has a right to expect thus much from every
one, and none should be drones but those who are incapable of becoming anything better.   It is the duty
of every man and unmarried woman to provide for
themselves according to the best of their abilities; and
what Dr. Arnold, the famous Rugby schoolmaster, said
of boys, is true also of girls—that the difference between one boy and another consists not so much in
talent as in energy; and it was his observation, that
those who became afterwards the most successful men
were not the cleverest boys, but the most hard-working
and energetic.

Mr. Samuel Smiles says that, "when a boy, he stood
in the same class with one of the greatest of dunces.
One teacher after another had tried his skill upon him
and failed; corporal punishment, the fool's cap, coaxing,
and earnest entreaty proved alike fruitless.   Sometimes
the experiment was tried of putting him at the top of
his class, and it was curious to note the rapidity with
which he gravitated to the inevitable bottom, like a lump
of lead passing through quicksilver.   The youth was
given up by many teachers as an incorrigible dunce,
one of them pronouncing him 'a stupendous booby.'
Yet, slow though he was, this dunce had a sort of dull
energy of purpose in him, which grew with his muscles
and manhood; and, strange to say, when at length he
came to take part in the practical business of life, he

* " Self-Help."

was found heading most of his old companions, and eventually left the greater number of them behind." The last time Mr. Smiles heard of him he was chief magistrate of his native town.

I myself knew a similar instance in a girl who used to attend the village school I sometimes visited, where she was thought dull by her companions and teachers, and occupied a low place in her class. After leaving school she learnt dress-making, but becoming tired of that or not succeeding in it, she determined to become a saleswoman in a shop. To prepare herself for the position she spent ten shillings in taking lessons in arithmetic, for though she had learned at school, she was not perfect in it. Then she went to a town where she got a situation in a small shop at low wages. The following year she got a better situation in a large shop, and attracted the attention of the owner by her good conduct. In a short time he made her head manager and book-keeper of a branch establishment he had, where she received a high salary, and the respect due to a person in a position of trust. For several years she held this situation, and ended by marrying very respectably, having doubtless a good sum of money laid by to begin housekeeping.

It sometimes struck me that when this young person returned to her native village for a holiday, her former companions must have felt surprised to see the success of the girl they had thought dull, while they who had thought themselves clever were so completely beaten by her in the race of life, and were still pursuing

comparatively unimportant and ill-remunerated employments. Her success was, in fact, owing to moral causes.
She began by acknowledging her ignorance and taking
lessons to improve herself; then she was contented to
begin with low wages and an inferior situation. Finally,
her diligence attracted her master's attention, and when
placed in a position of trust she continued careful and
painstaking.

A conceited, proud, or careless person would have
failed in the same position, and her success was due
not to the presence of great abilities, but to the absence of bad qualities from her moral nature; and the
absence of bad qualities goes a long way towards forming good sense, which is perhaps more a negative than
a positive quality. Persons who are not guided by
vanity, or temper, or jealousy, or a love of amusement,
will be guided by reason, and to be guided by reason is
to possess good sense. "Good sense," a French writer
says, " is more valuable than any other science or accomplishment that can be learned under the sun;" and
any one can possess good sense who chooses to do so,
because with God's help, they can prevent themselves
from being guided by evil feelings. This is the wisdom
promised " to the simple." "If any of you lack wisdom, let him ask of God, that giveth liberally and
upbraideth not, and it shall be given him." *

When called on to make an important decision, such
for instance, as to determine her course of life and the
trade or profession she is to enter upon, a young woman

* James' Epistle, chap. i. 5.

should not decide hastily; she should take time to consider, and lay the case before God, asking Him to give
her wisdom to decide right, and to help her to drive all
bad motives from her mind which might lead her wrong.
Then let her reflect calmly on the subject and decide,
and having decided, let her embark with energy in the
undertaking and go on with perseverance, remembering
the text, "Whatsoever thy hand findeth to do, do it
with all thy might," and constantly trying to free herself from bad feelings of every sort, that she may never
fall under their dominion, but may always continue to
be guided by good sense; for good sense is nothing
but reason, freed by God's grace from evil motives and
passions.

Sometimes a silly girl, whose reason is obscured by
idleness, seems to think that attention to order,
punctuality, and method, may be excused her on account
of her sex, and that she is less to blame than a man
would be, for failing in these particulars.   Such an idea
is a complete bar to success in life.

On many points a woman can seldom or never come
up to a man's standard, but there is nothing to prevent
her from equalling him in these essentials, and as she
cannot be useful in various other ways, in which he can,
she ought to endeavour to make up by increased
attention to these important details.   A woman can do
nothing well, which requires severe physical toil, but her
want of strength is no excuse for making awkward
figures and blots in account-books, or for unpunctuality
or want of politeness to customers.

A woman may sometimes be excusable for failing

through lack of knowledge or intelligence, as her
education may have been defective, but to fail through
want of care or painstaking is inexcusable. The girl
who fails thus does a serious injury to all other working
women, for by her folly she creates an unfavourable
impression against them, and acts as a warning to
employers not to engage persons of her own sex.
A woman should not, however, rest content with
inferiority in intelligence or knowledge; for though
such inferiority may be excusable, may not perhaps
be at all her own fault, she will always find it intensely
disadvantageous.   She should, therefore, endeavour
to supply her deficiencies by procuring instruction
before she begins on her work, unless, indeed, she
intends to be contented with a low salary; for if she
does not come up in these respects to the ordinary
standard of men, she will never be able to obtain a
high one.

Women sometimes fail on another point.   Their
nervous system being excitable, they are apt to betray
irritation at small vexations.   This infirmity happily
does not affect all women, or even the majority, but
they are more liable than men to become its subjects,
and ought therefore to guard with extra care against it.
Of all powers, that which increases the most with
exercise is self-control, and also there is no power so
easily lost by neglect.   A calm manner gives a great
advantage; it is an element of success; and to a
considerable extent it may be obtained by an effort, or
rather by a continual series of efforts, till at last it
becomes habitual.   Calmness always gives the im-

pression of superiority, for it is one of the signs of strength of character.

A woman who observes these rules, has good health, and avoids entering on a profession which is already over-crowded, will seldom fail of success.*

* Women so often fail from want of health, that a few observations on the subject will not be misplaced.

A girl's health is often injured by her being sent to school too young. Until a child is six or seven years old, the less it studies and the more it plays, the better. A tendency to curvature of the spine is frequently induced by sitting for hours on benches without backs, and is increased by sleeping always on the same side at night. Children will sleep with their faces towards the light, if only a glimmer comes through the window, and, therefore always lie on the same side; this is remedied by changing the pillow from the head to the foot of the bed every night, as is now commonly done in well-regulated nurseries.

When girls are grown up, they usually suffer from want of air and exercise, unless they have to go out as servants, and then they get too much work. Sometimes, in the same house, two girls are suffering from very different causes. The daughter of the house is out of health from want of exercise, while the poor servant-maid is injured by too hard work; if the former was good-natured enough to help the latter, she would be often rewarded by recovering her own strength and appetite, for household work in moderation is very wholesome, as it strengthens the muscles of the arms and chest.

Young-women are apt to stay at home, except in very fine weather, for fear they should spoil their clothes; but if they would put on woollen petticoats and tuck up their gowns, as the fine ladies do in Belgravia, they might go out without soiling anything, and a walk in rain under an umbrella is much better than no walk at all. An hour's brisk walking a-day is the least exercise a girl living at home should be contented with, and she will be the better for more, probably. When out in a situation she should make a point of getting at least half-an-hour's run before beginning the day's business, if it is of a sedentary kind, for air and exercise are the best preservatives of health and the only safe medicines. Tight lacing is a common cause of ill-health. Girls fall into this habit gradually, and are ignorant of the harm they are doing themselves. While still growing, a girl will have her gown let out everywhere except round the waist, which remains no bigger at eighteen than it was at fifteen, though every other part has grown larger. The pressure has increased so gradually that she has become used to it, and protests, with sincerity, that her clothes feel quite loose. The test of the truth of this protest is, whether she can lie down comfortably on her *side* while dressed; unless she can, she is too tight. Also, if she feels relief on taking off her clothes, or if she measures smaller round the waist when dressed than when undressed, in either case she is hurting her health—perhaps hurting it seriously.

CHAPTER III.

Choice of a Business, and Emigration.*

" We sincerely hope that a new system may be instituted at once, and that we may no longer see women who, like men, must needs often turn to labour for their bread, condemned, unlike men, to the ranks of one miserable and hopeless calling, or left with the single alternative of becoming, according to their positions, either distressed needlewomen or distressed governesses."—*Times, Nov.* 8, 1859.

"Obvious are the means of righting the labour market,—on the one hand by systematic emigration, and on the other hand by opening up new occupations adapted to women, and they must be such occupations as shall leave the woman—a woman still."—*Ultimate Civilization, by Taylor.*

THE choice of the occupation to be followed must mainly depend on the social position, education, and opportunities of each individual, but some hints may be useful as applying equally to all,

Those professions should be avoided which are already over-crowded. This is a truism; yet, strange to say, this plain rule is little considered by young women starting in life; for though it is obviously bad policy to embark in an underpaid employment, it is also difficult to get out of the beaten track.

* Part of this chapter has appeared in the "Englishwoman's Journal."

Perhaps no profession is more overcrowded than that of the teacher. One reason for this seems to be that there is no other profession open by which gentlewomen can earn their livelihood without loss of caste, and many prefer poverty to a loss of social position. It is impossible not to sympathize with this feeling; but while we sympathize we must also deplore it, because of the misery it occasions. Poor professional men often engage in a painful struggle to save the means by which their daughters are to be trained as governesses, and if enough can be afforded to give them such a thorough education as shall secure them good situations and high salaries, it is, probably, the wisest course that can be pursued. But if a second-rate education only can be afforded, then uncomfortable situations and a low salary are sure to fall to the daughter's lot, and the policy of the proceeding becomes more than doubtful.*

Would it not, under such circumstances, be wiser to bring them up to some less genteel but better remunerated employment, or to some humble department of their father's own profession? A poor solicitor might, for instance, teach his daughter to copy law papers, and set her up as a law stationer at a very small expense, and, once established, she would be able to keep on the business even after her father's death.

---

* This is peculiarly the case with regard to nursery governesses, of whom there is such an extraordinary surplus that it is scarcely possible to get a situation, and as young persons are always preferred, it becomes after thirty almost absolutely impossible. The salary diminishes as the nursery governess grows older, which is contrary to all other professions. Of all employments this is the worst, except needlework.

In the same way, an artist would have a good opportunity of starting his daughter as a wood-engraver, and so on.

Another reason for the overcrowding of the teacher's profession is, that young persons often enter it who are not gentlewomen by birth, for the sake of social advancement; just as men sometimes go into the Church or the army in order to become gentlemen by profession.

But, if any other employment is open to them, the young women mistake their own interest, for the satisfaction of being considered a lady can hardly make up for the many privations of a governess's life. Tradesmen's daughters often have the chance of engaging in commercial pursuits, and would do well to take advantage of any opportunity that occurs. This does not apply to persons who have a taste for teaching, as those who have a strong vocation for any profession are pretty sure to succeed in it. I speak only of ordinary women who have no particular vocation, and are equally ready to enter whatever employment seems to offer the greatest personal advantages.

The long list of pensioners at the Governesses' Benevolent Institution, and the still longer list of candidates for pensions, shows what a bad trade teaching is.*

* I am acquainted with two sisters, gentlewomen by education and manners, and perhaps by birth, too, who keep a bookseller's shop and circulating library, and drive a prosperous trade. The position of these ladies is certainly more comfortable than that of an ordinary governess. It appears to me to be also more dignified than the condition of the poor lady-pensioners aforesaid, and not to fall far short of the seldom-attained position of the teacher who has succeeded in realizing an independence.

Those, however, who intend to become teachers should endeavour to prepare themselves well for the position, both for their own sakes and that of their future pupils.

The Cambridge University Local Examinations, now open to girls, offer an excellent opportunity for preparation. Those who pass will receive certificates, and these certificates will be of great value as an assistance in obtaining good situations. Their money value will be great, for those who get them can ask higher salaries than others, besides which they will confer social consideration and respect. It is not necessary to learn Latin or Greek in order to pass. A good English education, with a knowledge of one foreign language, modern or ancient, and either music or drawing, is all that is required; these branches of knowledge must, however, be thoroughly learned or no certificate will be granted.

Parents who intend their daughters to be teachers, should send them to a school where young ladies are prepared for these examinations.

Dress-making is another over-crowded employment, and for much the same reason; dress-making being to persons in a certain position of life, what teaching is to those of the rank above them, viz., the most genteel occupation within reach. The wages of first-rate hands seem to have fallen about one-half in the last twenty years, and inferior workers have of course suffered in proportion. Yet, though everyone knows that there are far too many dress-makers, girls of the middle class beginning life seldom think of becoming anything else; they hope to succeed better than others; a few do well,

they think, and why should they not be among the few ?
Now, if a young person has no choice but to become a
dress-maker, she is right enough to enter on her work in
a cheerful spirit, and to hope for the best ; but if she
can avoid entering this employment, it is certainly her
interest to do so ; and this is especially the case if she
is a physically strong person ; for needlework, being a
sedentary employment, requiring little strength, is
peculiarly well suited to the feeble, but is injurious to
the muscularly strong, who require active exercise.
Nature here, as in many other instances, has pointed out
the proper division of labour, and punishes those who
infringe her rules by destroying their health.

It will, perhaps, be as well to mention some other
employments for women.   Professions connected with
literature and the arts need not be spoken of, as all who
'possess sufficient taste and talent will be sure to enter on
these agreeable avocations ; but I may observe that a new
branch of art is being opened to women—that of house-
decorators.   (See Appendix A.)   A lady of my acquaintance has had part of the woodwork of her house decorated
by them, with coats of arms and mottoes connected with
her husband's family.

Wood-engraving has already been mentioned, and I
am told by the superintendent of the Female School of
Art that as fast as the pupils become proficient they
obtain employment.

Photography is a good employment for women, though
it can seldom be well learnt without a regular apprenticeship, and the cost of materials before a person can set up
for herself amounts to at least £40.

Another good employment is the tinting of photographs. Any woman with an ordinary knowledge of painting in water-colours, whether portraits or flowers, could do it with a little practice. To make the photograph take the paint, it must first be washed over with gum-water, or silica,* which is better, and left to dry. The flaws must be covered with white paint; moist colours should be used. Some knowledge of art is required, to choose harmonious colours for the dresses and backgrounds, and of course the better the artist the more highly finished and the prettier the picture will be, but many women have sufficient knowledge and skill to attain to the art if they would buy a dozen common photographs to practise upon. It is an easy accomplishment, and as most people are discontented with their own photographs, and would like to have them improved, an artist of this kind would probably find plenty of customers.

Much success cannot, however, be expected unless the beginner can afford to spend a pound or two in advertisements. Work will then probably flow in, and if the artist is a good one, her paintings will recommend her; but whenever work falls slack, recourse should again be had to advertisements.

Photograph printing is also a good trade. Advertisements are of no use here. Persons who wish for employment, must take specimens of their printing round to photographers and ask for work.

* Silica, or glass medium, as it is sometimes called, can be procured from Miller's, 56, Long Acre. It is stated that by means of this material, plaster walls become easy to paint on, which opens a wide field to house-decorators.

A medical college for women has lately been opened. This is so new an institution that its success cannot be decisively spoken of. Several ladies have become pupils, and further particulars can be ascertained from the Hon. Secretary, 4, Fitzroy Square, London. W. C. There are said to be four hundred lady doctors in the United States, and there appears every reason to expect that the experiment will be equally successful here.

Nurses for the sick are scarce, many women of doubtfully sober habits being employed in that capacity through the difficulty of obtaining better. But this noble profession is suited only to persons possessing strong nerves and superior intelligence, as well as good health, and requires a peculiar cast of mind, combining force of character, good temper, and the power of being contented with little gaiety and amusement. Only a select few can therefore be fitted for it; but those who feel themselves suited for this employment could not engage in a more useful and honourable career. Midwifery is a good trade in large towns, and would be a still better one if educated women engaged in it.

A list of institutions, where women are taught midwifery, and trained as nurses, is given in Appendix B., with their terms. In a few of them, arrangements are made for receiving persons of superior station. The pay of nurses in some of these institutions is good, and occasionally retiring pensions are given.

The pay and treatment of nurses in government hospitals for soldiers is, however, better than in any private establishment, as the hours of work are much shorter, and good retiring pensions are provided.

Application should be made to the Lady Superintendent, Military Hospital, Netley, Southampton.

The copying of law papers, or law stationery, as it is usually called, is a very good profession for women, who unite a tolerable education to natural intelligence. Persons now engaged in this trade who were once daily governesses, have expressed a decided preference for their present employment. The average earnings of a clerk are from twelve to fifteen shillings a week, but very skilful hands can make more, and the head of an establishment realizes a far larger profit. Those wishing to learn the trade can be taught. *(See Appendix C.)* But it would be useless for anyone to try to set up for herself, unless she was assured of the patronage of two or three solicitors. Probably, however, solicitors have poor female relatives, like other people, and would be glad to provide for them in such a creditable and lady-like manner. The head of one of the establishments is the daughter of a solicitor.

It is needless to speak of clerkships in telegraph offices, as these situations are so sought after that there are far more candidates than vacancies. The kind-hearted gentleman, J. Lewis Ricardo, Esq., M.P., who first caused girls to be taught this trade, is recently dead, and women may well mourn his death, for in him they have lost a most efficient friend.

A good many young women are employed as assistant clerks in post offices, and sometimes in private business offices, to copy letters, &c. A good handwriting is the chief requisite; the power of making money calculations quickly and correctly is also needed, a point in which some women almost always fail, owing to their superficial and inaccurate education, and which, if they are wise, they will remedy by self-teaching, or by taking lessons in arithmetic, before they attempt to obtain a situation of the kind. Sometimes they are employed as book-keepers in shops. These situations are tolerably well paid. Several young women taught in a school in connection with the Society for the Employment of Women, have obtained situations as clerks and book-keepers, and given satisfaction to their employers. Several tradesmen have been so well pleased with the clerks first engaged that they have since engaged others.

Saleswomen in shops are generally well paid; it is a position that requires much bodily strength, because of the number of hours they have to stand; a good knowledge of arithmethic is also necessary, as indeed it is in almost all employments, but those of ill-paid drudgery. A good temper, or at least the power of self-control, are also requisite, to secure invariable courtesy towards the customers. The slightest want of politeness towards customers, even if they are themselves unreasonable and rude, is a breach of honesty towards the owner of the establishment; for if customers are offended they are likely enough to withdraw to some other shop. No one, therefore, should enter on this employment who does not possess entire self-command.

In all cases where a father with daughters keeps a shop, they should learn to serve in it, unless indeed he has already made his fortune, and can leave them comfortable independent incomes; for a daughter thus trained will always be able to earn her bread, and if

she have no brother, or if he enters some other profession, she will then be able to succeed her father in
the business, and will know how to carry it on.   This
is sometimes done, but not so often as it ought to be,
and the custom seems to be confined to some particular
trades, for which there appears no reason.   If women
have commercial ability enough to carry on the trade of
bookseller and baker, why should they not also be
grocers, drapers, silkmercers, hairdressers, &c.?   One
trade is probably not much more difficult to learn than
another, and the bookselling trade, which women often
engage in, is perhaps as difficult and complicated as any.
It is to be feared that this arrangement would be objected
to by the daughters themselves, partly from a love of
idleness, and partly because of the idea that to become a
tradeswoman is less genteel than to be a nursery
governess; the silly girls not perceiving that an independent position is, if not as dignified, at least much
more comfortable than that of a teacher, and that
whatever superiority a nursery governess may have in
point of gentility is more than counterbalanced by the
solid advantage on the other side.

   If girls would learn their father's business, it might
then, in cases where there is one son and one daughter,
be left to them as joint partners, as is often done when
there are two brothers.   But whether this was done or
not, the knowledge acquired behind her father's counter
would enable her to get good situations in other shops.
A girl should always consider it a great advantage to be
taught her father's trade, as she then learns under his
protection, is sure to be well taken care of if ill, and not

to be overworked. A photographic artist at Brighton has brought up his four daughters to his own business, and it is said the whole family are prospering. Such examples should be more frequently followed. The daughters are thus provided with a comfortable maintenance, and their father on his deathbed will have the comfort of reflecting that he has secured them from the evils and dangers of poverty.

There are several other handicrafts requiring skill rather than strength, in which women might very well engage, though they seldom do, and which they should beg their fathers as a favour to teach them.

From whatever cause it may proceed, it is certain that a lack of spirit and energy is often to be seen in women; they seem to be willingly helpless and contentedly inferior, as if they thought that God had made them so, and it was not their own fault. For example, I once went into a shop kept by a widow, in which there stood a weighing-machine where people were in the habit of getting weighed. I told the mistress I wanted to be weighed; she replied she did not understand the machine herself, but her "young man" would soon be back. Now the woman could have learnt the use of the machine by half an hour's study, but would not take the trouble, and thus left herself at the mercy of her assistant, for as all the heavy packages of groceries were weighed by it, it was perfectly in his power to cheat her.

This quiet acquiescence in ignorance and helplessness is melancholy to observe, and unhappily such instances are not uncommon.

In France, women have far more energy, and constantly undertake the whole management of shops.

At Dieppe they carve ivory brooches and other ornaments, and send them to England, where great numbers are sold, by which they must reap a little harvest.* Why should not English women pursue this easy and pleasant trade?

Great quantities of ladies' shoes are also imported from France, made by women, and sold at a very low price. English shoemakers should teach their sisters and daughters the handicraft, for why should foreigners enrich themselves while our own women starve?

For persons who have not had a superior education, and who have no chance of learning a handicraft, cooking is by no means a contemptible employment.

Formerly women could only become cooks by first becoming scullery and kitchen maids, and working up through a long course of drudgery; but now, by means of the cooking schools established in London, a person can at once begin at the top of the profession, and thus cooking becomes a trade fitted to a much higher class of persons than it used to be. (*See Appendix E.*)

Cooks' wages are never low, and are sometimes very high; they may be said to range from £16 a-year to £60, according to the skill of the performer. These cooking schools will also be useful to women who belong strictly

---

* Women in France also work as jewellers; polishing, setting, and imitating precious stones. This is probably the reason why French trinkets are so cheap and pretty. They are beginning to do mosaic work like the Florentines. In Switzerland women make watches, clocks, and spectacles.

to what are called the labouring classes, for many of them have not sufficient strength to go through the apprenticeship otherwise necessary in farm-houses and such like hardworking places, to prepare them for service in gentlemen's houses; but now, by paying a fee, they can be taught to cook, and can at once be made capable of taking good places.

There is another plan by which this useful profession might be made accessible to numbers now excluded from it. At present, families are generally supplied with cooks from the kitchens of people who keep larger establishments than they do ; thus the duke's kitchenmaid goes to the squire as cook, and the squire's kitchenmaid becomes cook to the village doctor or clergyman. But as there are many more small than large establishments, the supply is insufficient, and though nobody goes without cooks, women who know very little about cooking are often engaged, and ill-dressed dinners are the consequence.*

This might be remedied by introducing the apprentice system common on the Continent. It now often happens that a cook does not choose to teach her kitchenmaid much. Perhaps she is afraid that she might be engaged in her own stead if she grew skilful, or perhaps she is simply ill-natured, and does not choose to take the trouble, and so the poor maid gets little instruction. But if the cook was allowed to take an apprentice and to receive a fee for teaching her, she would take pains

* Teaching cookery will not cause a larger number of women to be employed, as nobody now goes without a cook; it will only improve the quality of the dinners.

D

to teach, and at the end of a year or two, would send
her out an accomplished cook.   This system works well
abroad, and there does not seem to be any reason why it
should not in England.   It would cost the mistress of
the house nothing but the food of the apprentice, and the
use of an extra hand in the kitchen would be worth that.
The cook would be glad to receive a fee, the apprentice
would be glad to learn, the kitchenmaid would hear the
instructions the cook was giving the other girl and pick
up a little knowledge by this means.   Thus all parties
would be benefited, and the race of cooks multiplied and
improved.   Two grades of cooks would then exist ;
those who began as scullerymaids and gradually worked
up from the lowest ranks, and those who became cooks
by purchase, paying a fee to learn.   These latter would
belong to a higher class than the former, and be more
fit to become housekeepers.*

Industrial schools will be of use in enabling many girls
to become servants who would otherwise have found it
impossible, for gentlefolks will not engage untrained
girls ; they must, therefore, get their training either
in industrial schools, or in hard places where the work
is severe, and the pay only just enough to supply them
with clothes.

Parents hardly seem sufficiently aware what a benefit
these schools will confer on their daughters, by enabling
them to avoid hard places.   If a young creature,
whether a horse or a human being, is over-worked in

* This plan is pursued in several London clubs. The head cook will,
on receiving a fee, take assistants who wish to be taught the higher
branches of the business.

its youth, it cannot recover entirely, and never becomes as strong and healthy as it would otherwise have been. Horse-flesh is so very valuable, that no one would think of setting a two-year-old to pull a cart, because of the injury that would be done it ; but it is not thought necessary to take so much care of girls, who are sent out to work hard while still growing, to their great future injury.

Some spirited ones, who will not give up soon enough, break down under it at once, and return home, perhaps to die, perhaps to be delicate for life, which for a working woman is the worst fate of the two. The very strong can stand this early hard work, but girls of average strength are hurt, and the weakly cannot bear it at all. But where industrial schools are established, this evil can be done away with, for girls taught in them will be able to get tolerably good places at once, and the knowledge of this will compel harsh mistresses to be more considerate to the poor young girls whom they employ ; for if they treat them ill, they will be unable to get any servant at all, as the girls will go to the industrial school to learn their business, rather than take a place where there is danger of being over-worked ; and in these schools they will learn much that is valuable besides. Habits of truthfulness and tidiness will be inculcated, and in many cases much that is evil in example may be avoided by keeping away from the wretched places to which girls are often compelled to go, to learn to be servants.

When once a girl has learnt enough of her business

to be able to take a place in a gentleman's family, the
life is far from disagreeable.   There is plenty of companionship to promote cheerfulness, and, if a woman is
careful, the wages are generally sufficient to enable her
to save a competence for her old age.   Some people
complain that maids' wages are too high; a most
unreasonable complaint, for surely a person who works
hard has a right to earn enough to keep her out of the
workhouse in her old age; and it does not appear to
me possible that this should be done under £14 or £15
a-year,* and even then it can only be effected by great
economy.   So far, then, from maids' wages being too
high, they are, in my opinion, almost lower than is
right; and ladies who endeavour to force them down
commit a great injustice.   The wages of an ordinary
woman with no particular skill ought to be sufficient
to enable her to provide for her old age, and those
who have skill besides, such as cooks and ladies' maids,
ought to be paid for it over and above.

Still compared to other employments for women, the
profession of a servant is a good one.   But some may,
perhaps, think that a needlewoman's life would be freer,
and prefer it on that account.   It is true that it is freer
in some ways, but the freedom is often dearly purchased.
In dressmaking establishments the hours of work are
fearfully long, frequently lasting from eight in the
morning till eleven at night, with only the necessary
intervals for meals.   No time for taking a walk on week

---

* A girl learning her business has, of course, no right to such high
wages, but only experienced women.

days, and no holiday but Sunday. This discipline soon destroys the health, and a girl with a strong constitution is often the first to fall ill.

Those, however, who prefer this trade in spite of its drawbacks, should take care to sew pretty well before they are apprenticed, or they will not give satisfaction. Parents who intend their daughters to be dressmakers should send them to schools where needlework is made a great object, that they may start with every advantage. It is hard on the head of a dressmaking establishment to be provided with an apprentice who cannot sew tolerably, and such incapacity is likely to make her not a little severe towards the unfortunate girl.

Plain needlework done at home is so ill-paid, that almost the worst kind of servant's place is preferable to this employment. The following is a list of the usual prices paid for needlework by the great shops and the contractors.

Ordinary gentlemen's shirts 10d. a piece (it takes twelve hours to make one); common men's shirts from $4\frac{1}{2}$d. to 3d., one firm gives only $2\frac{1}{2}$d. (two shirts may be made in ten hours); for heavy corduroy trousers, 6d. (a pair can be made in twelve hours); great coats, 7d. or 8d.

No class of needlework (except dressmaking) can be named which is not paid at the same inadequate rate, and thirty thousand women live by this trade in London alone. Thus the better class of workers receive 10d. a day, the inferior 8d., and the lowest 6d., out of which

thread has to be found.   Life on these terms is not life,
but a slow death.*

No one can live long on the diet necessitated by a
remuneration of 8d. or 6d. a day, when lodging, clothes,
fire, and candles have to be found as well. A strong
person may perhaps exist for a year or two, then a
cold or some slight ailment turns to consumption or low
fever, and she dies, and is entered on the death-rate
as dying of these diseases, but the real cause of death
was the previous low living, and want of the comforts
of life.

That women do so die instead of earning their living

---

* To show there is no exaggeration in this statement, the following
cases are given from the Report of the Needlewoman's Institution;
it will be seen that in some instances less is earned than is stated in the
text.

"Cases of previous low-paid labour among applicants for work at the
Society :—

"E. W. T. had worked for one shop five years—commenced at
5 A.M., worked till 11 P.M. Earned from 2s. 6d. to 6s. a-week,
according to the season.

"Mrs. M., bootbinder. Earns from 2s. to 4s. a-week for thirteen
hours' daily labour.

"M. B., widow, thirty years a needlewoman—no other means of
support. Makes shirts at 3½d. each, six button-holes in each. Can do
two a-day; finds her own cotton, light, and fire.

"H. R., works fourteen hours a-day at button-holes. Earns 4s.
a-week.

"J. C., an orphan and friendless, worked for four months for a con-
tractor at army braces; began at 7 A.M. and worked till 8 P.M.;
allowed half-an-hour for meals; when asked if that was time enough,
replied, with tears and sobs, 'Long enough, ma'am, for a crust of
bread; I'm only paid 2d. a dozen, and can't earn more than 2s.
a-week.' Had been a servant till ill health broke her down. Had
lived five years in one situation."

by wickedness is very true, and much to their honour;
that with the doors of a comfortable prison open
to them if they steal, they should not steal, speaks
highly for their good principles; they are as truly
martyrs as those who perish for their religion by the
hand of the executioner; in truth, their trial is longer
and more severe, for who would not find it easier to die
a public and speedy death, supported by the admiration
of friends and sympathizers, than to perish slowly and
obscurely as these poor creatures do? That many fail
in the ordeal is but to say that only a small percentage
of the human race are fit for martyrdom.

All who are wise will avoid this profession; not that
needlework is in itself a bad employment, on the
contrary, it is a very good one, but because such
numbers crowd into it, that the competition drives the
payment down to a point below that at which life cannot
for long be sustained.

All who have good feeling, all who love their neigh-
bour as themselves, will, if they have a chance, turn
to some other means of earning a livelihood, that their
unhappy sisters who have no other opening, no way
of escape, may have more room to struggle, and a
better chance of obtaining tolerable terms from their
employers.

There is an opening of which greater advantage
might be taken than is now done; that opening is
emigration. The colonies afford a wide field of well-
paid labour to certain classes of women. Domestic
servants of all kinds are wanted, especially cooks, not
the very best kind, but quite common ones get £30 and

£40 a-year, dairy-maids' wages are still higher, and
laundry-maids about the same. Maids of all work, in
England a despised race, there find themselves valued
and well-paid. This is true of all the Australian
colonies, but wages vary, and particulars of this sort
must be ascertained at the Emigration Offices. *(See
Appendix F.)* Government will often pay the passage
for able-bodied women, but a small sum, £1 5s. I
believe, is required for the outfit. It is said that women,
from an unwillingness to leave their country, often delay
in applying for a passage, till they are penniless,
thinking they can go at any time; then they find that
this sum is required, and not possessing it are compelled
to remain at home. Women should remember this, and
apply in time. Governesses are seldom required, the
supply already coming up to the demand.

The Government Emigration agent in Victoria, writes
on January 2nd, 1862, "No demand whatever exists
for the superior sort of emigrants, such as governesses
and milliners," and a Melbourne paper of several months
later, June 17th, 1862, confirms the statement. However, in some of the colonies a few governesses are
occasionally required, music being always an essential
qualification; and nursery governesses, who would not
object to help in household work, are in great demand,
and seem, from the accounts of those who have gone
already, to find the situations there agreeable. Such
persons and other educated women who may wish to join
friends, can obtain advice and assistance by applying to
the Middle Class Female Emigration Office, 12, Portugal
Street, Lincoln's Inn.

There is a great want of midwives, monthly and sick nurses, in the colonies generally, and specially in New South Wales. A lady, long resident at Sydney, says, that the pay of a monthly nurse is from £10 to £20 a month, besides presents ; there is such a scarcity that most unfit persons are frequently employed. This lady is of opinion that a sensible woman who could leech, apply blisters, dress slight wounds, &c., would find herself in great requisition, and be exceedingly well paid. Good handicrafts women, too, would probably find employment, such as ladies' shoemakers, hair-dressers, and makers of hair ornaments. These persons should take with them a box of tools, and materials, with specimens of their manufacture, which they should exhibit from house to house, asking for orders. Upholsterers, too, would be likely enough to make a good living ; but these last suggestions are my own idea only, I have no information on the subject. There are too many needle-women already.

Some months ago a proposal was made to send educated women in considerable numbers to the colonies, and a subscription was opened for the purpose. The public was appealed to, and money came flowing in, till a letter appeared in the *Times* from the Government Emigration Board, signed S. Walcott, which checked the stream. Mr. Walcott stated his belief that such persons were not wanted, and advised the benevolent to hold their hand, till the truth could be ascertained from the colonies. The colonial answers are conclusive. Canada, speaking through her emigration agent, Mr. Buchanan, says: "There exists but a very limited demand in this province for the class of women in question, and that the present introduction of such a class into Canada would be attended with consequences far from advantageous." Mr. Buchanan goes on to request the Emigration Commissioners that they will be pleased "to discountenance the emigration to this country of any grade of women higher than the domestic servant."

From Australia we hear in the *Melbourne Argus*, "There is no article, perhaps, in the labour market of less demand than governesses. There is no market, perhaps, where the value of educated women is less appreciated than in Melbourne." An agent of Adelaide confirms these statements, and information from the other colonies is all to the same effect.

Now, if this little history of the proposed emigration of educated women were not tragical, it would be comical. England so anxious to send them away, the colonies so afraid of having to receive them; England says to them, "Why don't you go to the colonies? you are not wanted here, you are burdensome to us, and we will gladly pay your passage to get rid of you."

The colonies hearing this indignantly exclaim, "For mercy's sake, don't send us such useless creatures! We want men to fell our woods, cultivate our land, tend our sheep and cattle, and women to cook our dinners, and wash our clothes, but as to educated women, we don't want them, and we won't have them; if they come they will be worse off than at home, for we have no workhouses to put them in." The injured attitude the colonies assume is amusing; they seem to regard the offer of a few hundred educated women to refine and improve them, as a fearful threat, and resent it, as people generally do resent suggestions that are intended for their improvement. But in fact all this is very sad, it is no joke to the poor creatures concerned, and it shows clearly how out of order some part of our social system must be, that such numbers of good respectable women should be at a discount, and of no use anywhere, a burden on every spot of earth, which people try to shift from one another, and which the inhabitants of each hemisphere wish were safely deposited in the other.

Possibly there may be several conducing causes to this strange state of things, but one in particular seems to me to stand out so clearly as the chief culprit, that I cannot refrain from calling attention to it. These educated women whom nobody wants, are educated in a general way, but *are not trained to any special trade or calling*. They know a little French, music, and drawing, but nothing well, nothing *professionally*. If these women had devoted all their powers since they were fourteen years old, to any *one* thing, leaving out all the others, they might have learned to excel in it, and been able to live by it. If one girl had learnt music exclusively, she might now have been able to play at concerts, and have been giving lessons at 10s. per hour; if another had devoted herself to painting only, she might have been able to live by selling pictures; or, if she had given herself up entirely to languages, she might have been able to earn her livelihood by translating books, or have been a foreign corresponding clerk in an office;

or, if she had only learnt writing and arithmetic, and
learnt them well, she might have been an ordinary clerk
or shopwoman; or, if her father had brought her up
to his own trade, she might be making ladies' shoes, or
riding-habits, or wigs, or selling groceries, or tuning
pianofortes, or gilding picture frames, or doing a dozen
other things, instead of living a burden to herself, her
friends, and her country. Poor creatures, the sins of
their fathers are visited heavily upon them! for they are
not to blame for the bad training they received as
children and young girls.

I believe the real cause of all this misery to be the
neglect of parents to apprentice their daughters to some
trade or handicraft, as regularly as they do their sons.
There is no reason why one sex should be more neglected
than the other, for no father would think of declining to
put his son to a trade, because an uncle might perhaps
leave him a fortune; neither ought he to think of not
apprenticing his daughter, because she may perhaps
marry, for as the *Melbourne Argus* truly says, "the
number of marriageable educated women in the world is
out of all proportion to the number of educated men,
who are prepared to marry them." If women were quite
positively certain to marry before their father's death, the
present system would not be so bad, but as they are not,
it is wicked and cruel, and based on a fallacy. Some
day the contrary principle will be universally admitted.
In course of time newspapers will take up the subject,
leaders will be written, and lectures given on the duty of
parents to their daughters; clergymen will preach about
it, and tracts will be distributed, and then it will be

recognized that a father who cannot leave his daughter a fortune, ought to teach her a trade, that she may be able to earn an honest livelihood ; and the man who fails to do this will be thought less well of by his neighbours. Then the position of women will begin to improve, and this superfluity of helpless, miserable creatures will gradually diminish till it ceases to exist.

Meanwhile, the only advice I can offer to the already existing superfluous women, who are too old to be apprenticed, is, that those who are fitted for it should become sick nurses, and that those who are not, but possess health and strength, should learn cooking and go into service, either here or in the colonies. I fear they will consider this a degradation ; but I do not see what else there is for them to turn to, and it is less degrading to live by honest work than to depend on charity. To those who have not strength for this, I can recommend nothing ; but the British public should remember that they are worthy objects of benevolence, for they are suffering, and suffering severely, more from the faults of others than from their own, and they belong to a class to whom life in a workhouse is more than usually irksome and painful.*

* A Society established in London, at 19, Langham Place, for promoting the employment of women, helps these poor creatures, by teaching them handicrafts and finding situations for them. It does some good, and would do more if its funds were larger. Post-Office Orders are payable to Miss Sarah Lewin, the secretary. The Society is also useful in detecting impositions, often attempted by advertisers, who offer to teach any woman some easy art on receiving a sum of money, and promising her employment in it afterwards. As a rule these offers are not to be trusted, though there may be exceptions. Before sending money the Secretary should be consulted.

CHAPTER IV.

Duty and Independence.

> How happy is he born, and taught,
>   That serveth not another's will ;
> Whose armour is his honest thought,
>   And simple truth his utmost skill.
>
> This man is freed from servile bands,
>   Of hope to rise, or fear to fall ;
> Lord of himself, though not of lands,
>   And having nothing, yet hath all.— *Wotton.*
>
> Oh ! what a world of vile, ill-favour'd faults,
> Look handsome in three hundred pounds a-year.
> > *Shakespeare.*

> A class (women) which needs all the safeguards that consciousness
> of independence can supply to protect them from moral dangers.
> > *A. Houston.*

IT is not easy to define what duty is, but one thing seems
pretty clear—that duties are reciprocal.

Thus a parent, who provides for his offspring in their
helpless childhood, has a right to expect that they will
in return provide for him when old age has made him
helpless. If they have the means of so doing and fail

to do it, they are undutiful. But if a parent deserts his child, and leaves it on a doorstep to the mercy of the passers-by, and some one should take it up, bring it home, and provide for it till it can work for itself, then the duty of that child is transferred to its chance protector; it will be bound to obey him in its childhood, and to help him in his old age, as if the adopted father had been the real one.

Thus duty partakes strongly of the nature of gratitude, and gratitude is a kind of justice—a return for favours received, the payment of a debt incurred. A duty performed calls for duty in return. If, therefore, a father has provided for his daughter in her childhood, she is bound to give him her obedience till she reach years of discretion, and this not grudgingly, but with goodwill and contentment, as she would pay a just debt. If a father has laid by a snug fortune for his daughter, and wishes her not to go out into the world to push her fortunes, but would rather she remained at home to amuse him and cheer him in his age, he would not be unreasonable in asking her so to remain, even if it was her wish to go out, for to lay by his fortune he must have deprived himself of many pleasures, many luxuries, perhaps many comforts; and for these sacrifices she ought to make some return. Care must, however, be taken to ascertain that the fortune thus saved is sufficient to provide for her according to her station in life, for if it is not, she must of course go out and work; as a woman should never run the risk of being driven into temptation through poverty. Her duty towards God is greater than that towards man, and if her father wishes

to place her in a situation of temptation she is bound to
disobey him. Even when there is no probability of
future poverty, the knowledge of a good trade is sometimes useful.

When the celebrated Madame de Genlis was compli-
mented on the variety of her accomplishments, she
replied that she prided herself more on knowing twenty
different trades, any one of which would procure her a
living.

When ruined and driven into exile by the French
revolution she found the use of this knowledge, for she
supported herself by the work of her own hands and
head for several years. Yet, when she learned these
trades, there did not appear to be any likelihood that
she would ever have required to earn her bread by their
exercise. Madame de Genlis was the daughter of a
merchant, the wife of a nobleman, and held a post of
importance about the royal family of France, but it was
her principle that every man and woman, whatever their
rank, ought to know how to maintain themselves in case
of unexpected misfortune. When, therefore, she was
appointed governess to the young princes and princesses,
the children of the king's cousin, she taught them
trades. One of the princes became an excellent carpenter, and another when in exile earned his living as a
teacher in a school. This prince afterwards became
King of France, under the title of Louis Phillippe, but
he was never ashamed of having worked for his living,
for he had been brought up to believe that usefulness is
always honourable.

She also taught the princesses trades, and besides,

took them to the hospitals to learn how to dress wounds, as she considered such knowledge to be becoming to women in all stations. If such principles were adopted in England a great improvement would soon be visible, but here the custom is widely different.

Parents, from a mistaken feeling of tenderness, are often too anxious to prevent their daughters from going out into the rough world. Sometimes a kind father says, " Why should my daughters go out to work ? As long as I live I will provide for them, they shall never come to want while I can work." This is very pretty, but the good man forgets he is mortal, that he may die at any moment, and that even if he lives to be seventy, his daughters, being younger than himself, will probably survive him. But, perhaps, he is sure that before he dies some one will marry them. Now he has no right to feel sure, because there is no certainty in the matter. The majority of women do marry, so he has a right to think it probable that his daughters will, but he is not justified in leaving their future well-being to a *probability*. He does not leave his own maintenance in old age to a probability. On the contrary, he carefully saves for it, buys, perhaps, a government annuity, and would feel wretchedly uneasy if it was only *probable* that he would not spend his own old age in the union workhouse. He should do by his daughters as he would have wished his own father to do by him, either providing them with a sufficient income out of his savings, or if this is not possible, having first given them the best education in his power, he should apprentice them to some trade, and send them out to learn to work for themselves while they

E

are still young, and he has still a home to offer them in
case of illness or casual want of employment. Then by
the time he dies they will have risen in their professions,
have saved money, and will be well able to maintain
themselves without his help. The result of not so
doing, but of trusting to probability, is well described by
a workhouse visitor. " If we compare the male and
female wards of the same workhouse, we shall usually
find among the latter a preponderance of cases of
reduced respectability and blameless destitution. There
are two or three women for every man in the same
predicament. And why? Not assuredly because women
are less thrifty than men, less industrious, or less
careful of their resources. Quite the reverse. As an
experienced friend once remarked to me, such an event
as a woman becoming bankrupt through her own fault
had never occurred to his knowledge; yet women are
driven by hundreds from comfortable homes to spend
their last days in the workhouse, because the men who
have assumed to provide for them have failed to do so,
and because no means are open to them to provide for
themselves."*

I may here remark that employers are unwilling to
take apprentices or untrained assistants after the age
of twenty-four, and in many trades and handicrafts
they prefer much younger ones. The sooner girls start
therefore to learn their business the better; they must
at least begin early enough to become experienced and
expert hands before they reach the fatal age of five-and-
twenty, at which period employers object to engage them,

* " Workhouse Journal," for September, 1861, page 483.

on the ground that they are too old to learn, or at least that they no longer learn with the facility of younger people.

A friend of mine who keeps a very miscellaneous register office for women, told me that she had comparatively little difficulty in finding places for the young girls on her books, but that the older ones troubled her. "Oh! my poor women of thirty," she cried, "I wish I could get places for them." Another bad result of trusting a woman's future maintenance to the probability of her marrying is, that it places her under a temptation to marry some one whom she does not like. If she does not marry she must end her days in the workhouse, so, if the man she likes does not propose, she is under a great temptation to accept the man to whom she is indifferent. Now, if she told the poor fellow honestly that she did not care a straw about him, he would beg to decline the honour of her alliance, so she is under the necessity of deceiving him; and as to deceive him during the time of courtship only would not answer, for if he found out the truth after he was married he would be terribly angry, she must continue to lead a life of hypocrisy, and deceive him all his days, thus steeping her soul in deceit.

The first prize in life is a happy marriage, the second a life of independence, the third and worst fate an uncongenial marriage. The pursuit of the second prize in no way prevents the winning of the first, for the second best can at any time be exchanged for the best whenever the opportunity occurs, but the possession of the second-best fate almost secures against having to

endure the third and worst. Richter, in a passage
translated by Carlyle, says, speaking of these interested
alliances, "Oh! my heart is more in earnest than you
think; the parents anger me who are slave-brokers;
the daughters sadden me who are made slave negresses.
Ah! is it wonderful that those who in their West Indian
market-place must dance, laugh, speak, and sing till
some lord of a plantation take them home with him;
that these, I say, should be as slavishly treated as they
are bought and sold? Ye poor lambs! And yet ye,
too, are as bad as your salemothers and salefathers.
What is one to do with his enthusiasm for your sex,
when one travels through German towns, where every
heaviest purse, every longest-titled individual, were he
first cousin to the Devil himself, can point with his
finger to thirty houses and say, 'I know not; shall it
be from the pearl-coloured, or the nut-brown, or the
steel-green house that I wed? open to customers are
they all.' How, my girls, is your heart so little worth
that you cut it like old clothes, after any fashion, to fit
any breast, and does it wax and shrink then like a
Chinese ball, to fit itself into the ball-mould or marriage
ring-case of any male heart whatever? 'Well, it must
be, unless we would sit at home and grow old maids,'
answer they, whom I will not answer, but turn away
from scornfully."*

Now, if the damsels who dwelt in these queer-coloured
German houses were possessed of independent incomes,
or knew how to earn their own livelihood, this scorn is

---

* "Extra leaf on daughter-full houses," by J. Richter.

well merited ; otherwise it is unjust, and they are rather deserving of compassion, for what would Richter have them do ?   What can they do, but cheat some simple-minded man into the belief that they are attached to him, and so persuade him to support them ?

It has been said that courage is the first virtue, because without it none of the others can be exercised ; much the same may be said of independence, without which the best intentions, the purest sentiments, the noblest motives are unavailing.   It is, therefore, the first duty of every woman to secure her own indepen-dence, if it has not already been secured to her by her parents ; for without it she cannot tell how low she may sink, or what sins she may be driven to commit.

CHAPTER V.

Money.—How to Waste it.—How to Keep it.

Not for to hide in a hedge,
　　Nor for a train attendant;
But for the glorious privilege
　　Of being independent.—*Burns.*

Neither a borrower nor a lender be,
For loan oft loses both itself and friend,
And borrowing dulls the edge of husbandry.
　　　　　　　　　　　Shakespeare.

It is observed by Mr. Smiles, in his book on "Self-Help," that "Although money ought by no means to be regarded as the chief end of man's life, neither is it a trifling matter, to be held in philosophic contempt, representing, as it does, in so large a degree, the means of physical comfort and social well-being. Indeed, some of the finest qualities of human nature are ultimately related to the right use of money, such as generosity, honesty, justice, and self-sacrifice, as well as the practical virtues of economy and providence. On the other hand there are their counterparts of avarice, fraud, injustice, and selfishness, as displayed by

inordinate lovers of gain ; and the vices of thriftlessness,
extravagance, and improvidence, on the part of those
who misuse and abuse the means entrusted to them.

Comfort in worldly circumstances is a position every
man is justified in striving to attain by every worthy
means in his power. It secures that physical satisfaction
which is necessary for the culture of the better part of
his nature, and enables him to provide for those of his
own household, without which, says the apostle, a man
is ' worse than an infidel.' Nor ought the duty to be
any the less indifferent to us that the respect which our
fellow-men entertain for us in no slight degree depends
upon the manner in which we exercise the opportunities
which present themselves for our honourable advancement in life. The very effort required to be made to
succeed in life is in itself an education, stimulating
a man's sense of self-respect, bringing out his practical
qualities, and disciplining him in the exercise of
patience, perseverance, and such-like virtues. The
provident and careful man must necessarily be a thought-
ful one, for he lives not merely for the present, but
with prudent forecast makes arrangements for the
future."

Every one of these observations applies to women
as well as to men, and Mr. Smiles's remarks on the
whole subject of money, making and spending, are so
excellent, that I shall continue to quote them, only
begging my readers to add mentally the word "woman"
wherever "man" appears.

" Economizing one's means with the mere object of
hoarding is a very mean thing, but economizing for the

purpose of being independent is one of the soundest
indications of manly character." Manly here means
honest and brave, and in that sense it is a good thing
when women are "manly." "When practised with the
object of providing for those dependent on us it assumes
quite a noble aspect. It is the exhibition of one of
the best forms of self-help." Francis Horner's father
gave him this good advice on entering life :—"Whilst
I wish you to be comfortable in every respect, I cannot
too strongly inculcate economy. It is a necessary virtue
to all; and however the shallow part of mankind may
despise it, it certainly leads to independence, which is
a grand object to every man of a high spirit." "Every
man," continues Mr. Smiles, "ought so to contrive as
to live within his means. This practice is of the very
essence of honesty. For if a man do not manage
honestly to live within his own means, he must necessarily be living dishonestly upon the means of somebody
else. Those who are careless of personal expenditure,
and consider merely their own gratification, without
regard for the comfort of others, generally find out the
real uses of money when it is too late. Though by
nature generous, these thriftless persons are often driven
to do very shabby things; they dawdle with their
money as with time, draw bills upon the future, antici-
pate their earnings, and are thus under the necessity
of dragging after them a load of debts and obligations,
which seriously affect their action as free and independent men. The loose cash, which many persons throw
away uselessly and worse, would often form a basis of
fortune and independence for life. These wasters are

their own worst enemies, though generally found among
the ranks of those who rail at the injustice of the
world.   But if a man will not be his own friend, how
can he expect that others will?   Orderly men, with
moderate means, have always something left in their
pockets to help others, whereas your prodigal, careless
fellows, who spend all, never find an opportunity for
helping anybody.   *   *   *   *   *

"The proverb says, that 'an empty bag cannot stand
upright,' neither can a man in debt.   Debt makes
everything a temptation.   It lowers a man in his own
self-respect, and renders him a slave in many respects,
for he can no longer call himself his own master, nor
boldly look the world in the face.   It is also difficult for
a man who is in debt to be truthful, hence it is said
that 'lying rides on debt's back.'   The debtor has to
frame excuses to his creditor for postponing the payment
of the money he owes him, and also probably to contrive
falsehoods.   It is easy enough for a man who will
exercise a healthy resolution to avoid incurring the first
obligation : but the facility with which that has been
incurred often becomes a temptation to a second ; and
very soon the unfortunate borrower becomes so entangled
that no late exertion of industry can set him free.   The
first step in debt is like the first step in falsehood,
almost involving the necessity of proceeding in the same
course, debt following debt, as lie follows lie.   Haydon,
the painter, dated his decline from the day on which he
borrowed money.   He realized the truth of the proverb—
'Who goes a borrowing goes a sorrowing.'   The written
advice he gave a youth on entering the navy was as

follows :—' Never purchase any enjoyment if it cannot
be enjoyed without borrowing of others. Never borrow
money; it is degrading. I do not say never lend, but
never lend if by lending you render yourself unable to
pay what you owe, but under any circumstances never
borrow.' "

Dr. Johnson held that early debt is ruin. His words
on the subject are weighty, and worthy of being held in
remembrance. "Do not," said he, "accustom yourself
to consider debt only an inconvenience, you will find it
a calamity. Poverty takes away so many means of
doing good, and produces so much inability to resist evil,
both natural and moral, that it is by all virtuous means
to be avoided. * * * * * * *
Let it be your first care, then, not to be in debt to any
man. Resolve not to be poor; whatever you have,
spend less. Poverty is a great enemy to human happiness; it certainly destroys liberty, and it makes some
virtues impracticable, and others extremely difficult.
Frugality is not only the basis of quiet, but of beneficence. No man can help others that wants help himself;
we must have enough before we can spare."

These observations of Dr. Johnson's ought to be laid
to heart by every working woman; he explains so well
that the use of money, as soon as our own necessary
wants are provided for, is beneficence; and he also shows
so clearly that we must not attempt to help others, until
we have enough for ourselves.

It may, perhaps, be useful to enter somewhat more
into detail on these points, and to try to mark out how
far a single woman is bound to help her own family.

Her parents are, of course, her first duty.   If by
misfortune, or even by their own fault, they fall into
poverty in their old age, she must not desert them.
The care they bestowed on her childhood, must now
be bestowed on them.   If the daughter be alone in the
world, with no brothers or sisters to help her, the whole
weight of the charge falling on her, may prove too much
for her strength : in that case, though bound to support
them if in her power, she may be compelled to make
them over to the parish authorities ; but even then, her
care for them ought not to cease, and she should not fail
to provide them with such little luxuries and pleasures as
her means may afford.   If there are several brothers
and sisters, they are all bound to contribute their share
towards the support of their parents, according to their
salaries and incomes.

A son ought not to say that he has a wife and
family to provide for, and that, therefore, he must be
excused from contributing.   He had a father and
mother before he had a wife, and ought not to have
taken one, if so doing was likely to prevent him from
helping to support his parents.

A married daughter should contribute if her husband
will allow her, but not otherwise, as what a man earns,
or possesses, ought to be spent only according to his
wishes, and with his full knowledge and consent.

If she possessed money of her own before she married,
the obligation is, of course, stronger ; she is then
positively bound to assist them ; but it may not always
be in her power to do so, as, unless some provision was
made to the contrary at the time of her marriage, the

law gives the husband power over his wife's fortune and earnings, so that she cannot dispose of the least part of them even to assist her parents. On this account it is the duty of every woman with money, who has an old father or mother, or a crippled and helpless brother or sister dependent on her, or who may possibly become dependent on her, to keep her fortune in her own power, which is done by having a legal paper drawn before the marriage, settling it on herself, for her own sole use, and by appointing trustees to see that the arrangement is carried out, which any lawyer will know how to do correctly.*   Otherwise, a daughter might find

---

* The money must be invested in the name of the trustees, who will receive the interest and pay it over to the wife, who can then spend it according to her own wishes. The marriage settlement of the Princess Alice, now Princess of Hesse, is an instance of this arrangement. The clause runs thus :—"Her Britannic Majesty promises to secure to her royal highness the Princess Alice Maud Mary, from the time of her marriage to her royal highness's decease, the annual sum of £6000 sterling, to be paid quarterly to commissioners named for that purpose by her Britannic Majesty, to be by them received for the sole and separate use of the said Princess, notwithstanding her married state, and which annual sum of £6000 sterling, so payable quarterly, the said Princess shall not have power, either separately or conjointly with his Grand Ducal Highness the Prince, to alienate, mortgage, or receive or direct to be paid by way of anticipation ; but the same shall, from time to time, as the same shall become due, be paid and payable into the proper hands of the said Princess alone, upon her own sole receipt, or to such person or persons to whom she shall by writing signed by herself alone, from time to time, as the same shall, become due, direct and order the same to be paid, or whom she shall otherwise authorize to receive the same on her sole behalf." In making this settlement the Queen sets a noble example to all other parents. The opinion of the late lamented Prince is also here probably represented, that married women are the happier for an independent income.   In all

herself in the painful position of wishing to help her parents, yet being unable to do so, her own fortune earned, perhaps, by their toil, being no longer at her disposition.   When a woman has no one depending upon her, she is, of course, under no obligation to make this arrangement (though she will be . wise to make it); but she ought not to fail to do so, if the happiness and comfort of some poor helpless being rests on her having the power to aid them, for though three men out of four would willingly assist their wives' parents and helpless relations under such circumstances, the fourth might not consider himself bound to do so, and much misery might be the consequence.   Parents also ought to make the arrangement for their daughters, as it is always wrong to trust, without reservation, the happiness of a fellow-creature, much more of a daughter, to what is called "the goodness of human nature," for the simple reason that human nature is not perfectly good, and if perfect confidence is placed in it, it is apt to fail under the temptation thus put in its way.   The goodness of human nature when not assisted by strong natural

---

cases where it is wished to leave money by will to a married woman, it should be specified that it is for her " sole use," otherwise the husband will get it instead of the wife, and trustees should be named to see that this direction is carried out.   A lady of my acquaintance was, in consequence of the omission of a relative to take this precaution, reduced to extreme poverty in her old age, and if it had not been for the kindness of another relative, who gave her a small annuity, she must have appealed to charity, or have gone to the workhouse, her husband having spent every shilling belonging either to himself or to her before he died, although she had a large fortune besides the legacy, and he himself a large professional practice.

affection, (and it is well known that affection changes,)
is about as insecure a basis for happiness as can well be
imagined.　If human beings were perfectly good, they
might be perfectly trusted; but as they are only
partially good, they ought to be only partially trusted.

Among the highest classes, some arrangement to
protect the wife's interests is invariably made.　No
man of rank would approve of a marriage for his
daughter in which her interests were not protected by
settlements; nor, indeed, would the daughter think of
marrying a man who had so little regard for her as
not to suggest them, that is, without having her own
fortune, or an equivalent for it, sometimes if the husband is rich, with an addition to it out of his own
property, but at any rate, her own fortune, tied up, so
that the capital cannot be spent, to serve as a maintenance for her after his death, in case she should be
the survivor.

Besides this, the interest of her fortune, or a part of
it, is usually, though not invariably, settled on her to
be spent as she pleases during her husband's lifetime;
and this allowance, which is called pin-money, belongs
sacredly to her, and cannot be touched even by her
husband's creditors.

Often has this pin-money, together with the settlements, proved the means of saving a whole family
from beggary, for when a foolish man has run through
his own fortune, he is thus prevented from doing the
same by his wife's, and her pin-money serves to support
the family, and keeps them out of the workhouse.

It is much to be regretted, that this plan is not

generally adopted in all classes; it is a pity that an arrangement, which so greatly conduces towards the happiness of women, and is so advantageous to the whole family, should be confined to one class of the community only. Probably, the cause is a wish to avoid law expenses; but, in truth, the tenth part of a woman's fortune would often be well spent in securing the remainder to her own use, if only on account of the domestic harmony and absence of bickering which the arrangement produces. Even when husbands are prudent and trustworthy, a small independent income is found to be a great comfort to married women; it averts many a matrimonial dispute, and thus has a strong tendency to increase married happiness and domestic affection.

Lord Brougham, and several other eminent lawyers, are anxious that a law should be enacted, which would have the effect of giving settlements and pin-money, without legal expense, to every married woman with property of her own. Probably, this law will at some distant future time be passed, but until it is, every careful father and mother ought to provide their daughters with these resources, if they give them a fortune, in spite of the expense, whenever the arrangement is possible, for, in consequence of neglecting this precaution, sad misery is often inflicted.

To return to the obligations of a single woman towards her family. The claims of crippled or helpless brothers and sisters are, of course, as strong on single women as on married ones, and, to their honour, are seldom disregarded; indeed, claims which are sustained by early affection are generally well observed. Often is a poor struggling woman the support of an idiot sister or suffering brother; and to these sacred claims is often sacrificed the hope of earning a competence for her own old age. In that sad record of suffering, the list of candidates for pensions from the Governesses' Benevolent Institution, case after case is recorded of candidates who have saved nothing, having "supported a blind sister" or "a crippled brother;" and in every class of workers, the same glorious instances of self-sacrifice probably occur, though they pass unrecorded in other professions.

But though self-sacrifice, under such circumstances, becomes one of the highest and noblest virtues of our nature, there are other cases in which it ceases to be a virtue at all, and becomes a weakness : for, like all other virtues, it degenerates into a fault, unless subject to the principle of justice. To help those who cannot help themselves is just, but to sacrifice one-self to help those who ought not to require aid, is unjust and weak. Our rule of conduct is given in Scripture, "Let him who hath two coats, give to him who hath none." Yet often is the rule disregarded by women, who strip off their only coat to give to him who hath two already.

The Governesses' list of candidates again shows this. Often the record appears "lent all her savings to her brother," or "nephew, who became bankrupt." When women are asked by their relations to lend them money, to embark in a "perfectly safe business, which is sure to return a high interest," they should remember that if the statement was true, and the speculation was really a good one, business men, who understand the matter, would be glad to invest their money in it, and there would be no necessity to come borrowing. Yet the relation who says this, has probably no intention of cheating the woman whose money he fain would borrow; he believes in the speculation, and embarks his own money fearlessly in it. He holds up his single opinion against that of all other business men, who tacitly express their dissent from his views, by declining to adventure their money with him; and he expects his female relatives to have as much confidence in his judgment as he himself has, and will probably resent a refusal to lend as a personal affront, and a quarrel is likely enough to ensue. A woman thus urged should firmly decline, good-temperedly if possibly, but at any rate firmly; and if a quarrel be the inevitable result of a refusal, she must make up her mind to quarrel; for it is better to quarrel than to be ruined. If the idea enters her mind that she ought to yield, because self-sacrifice is a woman's part, she should remember what is said on this subject by a man whose learning and position make him very high authority.* "It is no doubt true that we should all be prepared, when necessary, to make great sacrifices of our feelings and interests to promote the good of our fellow-creatures. But that any one portion of humanity should be more particularly called upon than another to perform this act of self-immolation is, it seems to me, a most absurd and

* Arthur Houston, Professor of Political Economy at Dublin University, "On the Emancipation of Women from Iudustrial Disabilities," page 11. , (Longman,)

F

abominable doctrine. It is one of which those who are
called upon to make the sacrifice must feel the injustice,
and at which they must repine, unless where the vanity
of martyrdom—not so uncommon a vanity as may be
supposed—buoys them up under the trial. It is a
doctrine, too, which can have no other effect on the
remainder of humanity than to feed their arrogance and
minister to their selfishness. Self-sacrifice, to be
beneficial, must be a mutual duty."

Women who give up what is just from this mistaken
notion, are either trying to make themselves into
heroines, or else, which is the more common case, they
are cowards who yield, from the fear of offending, that
which in their hearts they had rather withhold. But
such concessions, for the sake of peace, are not always
likely to answer their purpose, if another distinguished
man is to be believed.* He says, "Never lend money
to a friend unless you are satisfied that he does wisely
and well in borrowing it. Borrowing is one of the most
ordinary ways in which weak men sacrifice the future
to the present, and thence it is that the gratitude for a
loan is so proverbially evanescent, for the future
becoming present in its turn, will not be well satisfied
with those who have assisted in doing it an injury.
By conspiring with your friend to defraud his future self,
you naturally incur his future displeasure.   *   *
    *   * ` *   *   To withstand solicitations
for loans is often a great trial of firmness; the more
especially as the pleas and pretexts alleged, are generally

* H. Taylor, in "Notes on Life," p. 26.

made plausible at the expense of truth.   *   *   *
The refusal which is at once the most safe from
vacillation, and perhaps as little apt to give offence as
any, is the point-blank refusal, without reasons assigned.
Acquiescence is more easily given in the decisions of a
strong will, than in reasons which weak men, under the
bias of self-love, will always imagine themselves competent to controvert."

The lady in whose school I was educated retired from
business late in life, with a good fortune, acquired by
her own exertions, intending to pass the evening of
her days in rest and comfort.   Unfortunately she was
induced to entrust her whole fortune to a promising
nephew.   He lost it all, and she was reduced to such
distress that she had to appeal to the charity of her
former pupils.   She ended by obtaining a situation as
companion, and is now dead.   The fate of this poor
lady ought to serve as a warning to all other women who
have laid by money.

Post-office savings' banks are the best places for a
woman's savings.   They receive to the amount of thirty
pounds a-year, and few indeed are they who can save
more; these few will do wisely to deposit the thirty
pounds there, and only risk the remainder in some other
investment.   Then, when work is past and the time for
rest has come, a Government annuity can be bought
with the money which has been placed in the savings'
bank.   The interest on these annuities, being for life
only, is very high and is perfectly secure, the Government being responsible for its payment, so that nothing
but a revolution, or the conquest of the country by a

foreign force, could prevent it from being paid. A woman of fifty-five may obtain an annuity of £10 for £140 5s. 10d. An annuity of £20 would of course cost twice as much. The older the person buying the annuity the less it would cost. At sixty it would be £122 15s. In many cases it may be well, however, to hold back a small portion of the savings, and not invest all in the annuity, because on the death of the annuitant the principal goes to the Government, and few people would like to be able to leave nothing behind them. Some relative, or friend, or faithful servant may have claims which it would be unjust and unkind to disregard.

Government annuities can now be bought at most of the chief Post Offices. This is a great accommodation to the public, and an especial comfort to single women, retired governesses, and old servants.

The Governesses' candidate list shows another very common way in which single women spend their earnings. The entry frequently appears, "has saved nothing, having educated her orphan nephews and nieces." The women who thus spend their earnings intend to do what is right, and therefore deserve our respect, but they have mistaken the means. To give an expensive education to nephews and nieces is wrong, when the aunt is thereby compelled to depend on the aid of a charity, or to come upon the rates; for then she has in fact educated her nephews and nieces out of other people's pockets, and it is the rate-payers and sub-scribers to the charity who pay for their education, not herself. Thus, she commits an injustice towards the

public.   Neither is her kindness towards her nephews
and nieces well judged, nor has it the effect of adding
to their happiness, but the contrary.   It is evident that
the education bestowed upon them has not enabled them
to earn comfortable incomes, or they would scarcely have
left the aunt to whom they are indebted for it to the charity
of strangers; and it is probable that their education,
though procuring it has ruined their aunt, has barely
afforded them the means of living.   The nephew is,
perhaps, a clerk, earning a hundred a-year, yet obliged
to dress and live like a gentleman, or perhaps a shopman
earning eighty; when, if his aunt had caused him to be
apprenticed to a handicraft, he might have been earning
ten or twelve shillings a-day in the colonies as a
carpenter or stonemason; and in British Columbia, and
some other colonies, the wages are much higher than
this.   Thus, he would be a far richer man, able probably
to help his aunt, and his life would be passed in the open
air, taking active exercise, instead of in a close office or
shop, from which his health is sure to suffer, even if the
confinement does not lead to habits of drinking and
dissipation, as it so often does; he would also be a free
man, able to please himself and be his own master in
all things, instead of being under the obligation not to
marry, a condition to which shopmen are usually
compelled to submit by their employers.   The case
with a niece is equally strong.   The education she
receives, though expensive, does not probably enable her
to become anything more than a second-rate governess,
earning a small uncertain salary; but if she had been
apprenticed to a good trade, or taught cooking in the

best style, she might have earned as good wages, and
from not being expected to dress like a lady, could have
saved more.   This education would cost but a tenth part
as much as a general one, and would make the niece a
much happier woman, less polished, and less learned,
but richer and freer.   It is a mistake to bring people up
to refinement, when the refined get worse paid than
unrefined workers.   It is unwise to spend money in
giving an education, the only effect of which will be to
disqualify the pupil for earning a good livelihood.   The
vague general education which has no effect, except in
giving refinement, is very much worse than useless ; for
refinement without the power of earning one's bread only
increases the evil of the position by making it the more
acutely felt.

Some women, however, reduce themselves to an old
age of poverty and dependence, by means less creditable,
and without the excuse of natural affection.   There is a
dreadful ambition abroad to be " genteel;" appearances
are too often kept up at the expense of future comfort,
and though we are not rich, yet we cannot be contented
without seeming so.   "We must be *respectable*," observes
Mr. Smiles, " though only in the meanest sense, in mere
vulgar show.   We have not the courage to go patiently
onward in the condition of life in which it has pleased
God to call us ; but must needs live (and dress) in some
fashionable state to which we ridiculously please to call
ourselves, and all to gratify the vanity of that un-
substantial genteel world, of which we form (or wish to
form) a part.   There is a constant struggle for front
places in the social amphitheatre, in the midst of which

all noble self-denying resolve is trodden down, and many fine natures are inevitably crushed to death."

How many a woman who might have lived happily by going on with her father's shop, has thrown away this comfortable reality from the vague notion that some other occupation would be more "genteel," and has thus exchanged easy circumstances and independence, for dependence and poverty?

I need not describe what other evil effects arise from this silly ambition to dazzle others with the false appearance of great worldly success—we perceive them around us in bankruptcy, poverty, and waste; but perhaps the most melancholy result of all is to see a youth and middle age of frivolity and extravagance, followed by an old age of penury, discontent, and dependence. When we see how happy women are who have achieved independence and earned for themselves a snug little income, and observe with what consideration and respect they meet in their own families, one regrets to see the means of procuring so much quiet contentment thrown away. Few positions to which a woman can attain, are happier than that of a single woman with enough for herself to live on comfortably and a little to spare for her friends. She meets with the genuine respect her successful exertions in life deserve, and if she is of a friendly disposition, and willing to lend a helping hand to the rising generation where help is merited, she will meet with affection and gratitude as well as respect. Such a calm pleasant evening to life is surely an object worth trying for. A youth of work and independence, and an old age of kindliness and usefulness, surrounded by the respect of contemporaries, who know our history, and the affections of the young who have benefitted by our assistance, is not a bad prize to draw in the lottery of life.

> "Jog on, jog on, with cheerful heart,
>   With Heaven's smile beaming o'er us,
> To cheer us in our daily work,
>   And light the path before us.

> "Then strength will be a strength indeed,
>   And labour a sweet pleasure:
> And doing what is fair and right,
>   The greatest earthly treasure."—*Broome.*

CHAPTER VI.

Self-Respect.—Example.—Influence.

> But where ye feel your *honour* grip
>   Let that aye be your border :
> Its slightest touches, instant pause,
>   Debar all side pretences ;
> And resolutely keep its laws,
>   Uncaring consequences.—*Burns.*

> Lives of great men all remind us
>   We can make our lives sublime;
> And departing, leave behind us
>   Footprints on the sands of time.—*Longfellow.*

> Speak gently, it is better far
>   To rule by love than fear ;
> Speak gently, let not harsh words mar
>   The good we might do here.—*Hymn.*

IT is not easy to define self-respect. Perhaps it is not a very bad definition to say that it consists in believing that God has given one a noble nature, and in a determination to do nothing unworthy of that nature. But though difficult to describe what it is, it is easy to show what it is not. It is not vanity, for vanity is ever seeking for applause and admiration, which self-respect

forbids.   It is not conceit, for conceit makes people
think themselves cleverer and handsomer than they really
are, which self-respect does not.   It is not pride, for
pride is quick to take offence, and self-respect is slow.
Yet pride is somewhat allied to self-respect: perhaps
pride is self-respect, mingled with and spoilt by vanity,
till half its good qualities are destroyed, or changed into
bad ones.   Vanity, however, has no relationship whatever
to self-respect.   They are deadly foes, and can scarcely
exist in the same disposition.   In fact, one is sure to be
smothered and crushed down by the other till its power is
hardly felt; and a character will be great or small, strong
or weak, imposing or frivolous, according to which of the
two opposing qualities gains the victory, and becomes the
ruling power of life.

Vanity in everything refers to the opinion of others,
what they will say or think, wondering whether that
action or this observation will meet with applause or
disapprobation.   Thus a vain character is seldom consistent, for sometimes it will seek to please one set of
people, then another, and different means must be used
for each; so it is ever changing, ever varying, and from
lack of perseverance seldom excels.   But self-respect
refers to no one, and goes its own way, contented if it
secures its own approbation and the respect of its fellow
men and women.   Yet it is not conceited, for its require-
ments are high, and it will never be satisfied till it comes
up to its own standard of excellence.   I have read an
anecdote which well illustrates the power of self-respect
in a child.   His companions laughed at him for missing
an opportunity of stealing some apples, when there was

no one to see him; "But," said he, "some one *was* there to see me : *I* was there to see *myself!*"

Self-respect is ever willing to learn, for it wishes to improve, and is not ashamed to own that it is ignorant. Vanity would be also glad to learn, that it may adorn itself with knowledge ; but then it cannot learn, without first betraying that it is ignorant, and that it could not endure. Vain people will deny a fault which they know they have committed to hide it from the world, but habitually self-respecting men or women will confess a fault or error if they are convinced they have committed it ; for to have done so is, they feel, unworthy of them, and they will make reparation as far as possible by confession, without considering what bystanders may think, for, till they have done so, they cannot forgive themselves or regain their self-respect. This good quality, which more than any other will preserve those possessing it from mean faults, is in the power of every one to acquire, for in good truth God *has* endowed each one of us with a noble nature, or at least with the germ of a noble nature which if we choose to cultivate, and do not allow to be overrun and smothered by that vile weed, vanity, will grow into a great tree bearing good fruit.

One of the good fruits it will produce is peace, for self-respect is not quarrelsome ; it will not dispute where it is in the wrong, and it will be careful never to advance unjust claims, preferring rather to give up a just right, than to enforce a doubtful one. Neither has self-respect any tendency towards insubordination, for self-respect is ever ready " to give honour where honour is due," and to obey lawful authority. It has been remarked that proud women make the most obedient wives. This is readily to be believed, for by pride is here meant self-respect; and self-respect forbids to break a promise, or to evade it, though it will not rashly make one. All employers have lawful authority over the employed, as long as they keep to the terms of the agreement; a self-respecting person will therefore carefully obey her employers, and punctually carry' out their directions, unless, indeed, they break their agreement, and then she will manfully resist them. The senseless "Uppishness," to use a vulgar but expressive word, sometimes seen in young girls towards their employers, has nothing to do with this quality, but is allied to vanity, as its usual object is a false display of spirit, to produce an effect on beholders; and such displays are not unfrequently followed by an abject submission, entreaties for pardon, and tears. But a self-respecting person will never draw the sword except in a just cause, and when peace can no longer be maintained without a sacrifice of principle; and then she will be ready to sheath it again whenever fair and just terms of agreement are offered.

Self-respect is a great foe to jealousy, that child of vanity still meaner and more contemptible, because more malignant, than its parent; for self-respect, valuing itself highly and knowing its own worth, is not sorry to see others valued and honoured also. Jealousy is not only mean, it is foolish; for the race of life is long, and the best runner is sure to win at last, not the fastest runner always—for a fast runner may fall, or go on the wrong side of the post and have to come back again—but the best, the steadiest, the most enduring, who takes care not to fall, and to keep in the right course. Though others may get the start at first, such a runner is sure to win. Whoever feels himself to be such a runner may make sûre of the prize, but if the best runner does not happen to be one-self, but some one else, why should we be angry at his success? It is right and just that the most meritorious should get the prize, and the person who grumbles at losing it is unreasonable.

The world is seldom unjust in its estimate of character, though individuals often are. Not, indeed, that individuals even are unjust to striking merit—that is acknowledged everywhere—but to obscure, yet real merit. Thus, in a small circle, a meritorious person may be overlooked and undervalued. It is not that the individuals composing it mean to be unjust—for every one intends to be just, when his own interests are not concerned—but because they are stupid, and cannot perceive merit unless it is very obvious, and also perhaps because they are deluded into admiring some brilliant imitation which for a time they mistake for the real thing.

When this is the case, let the undervalued person move, if possible, into a fresh circle; but if the same phenomenon renews itself, if worth is again left languishing unnoticed in a corner, let a suspicion enter the head of the unappreciated individual that she is not so very worthy after all, and that she only meets with the treatment she deserves. There is a French saying, " *Tout le monde a raison*," "All the world is right;" and if a person is continually finding herself undervalued, why, then, the simple fact is, that she overvalues herself, and that the other people are right.

So, instead of complaining, let her set to work to make herself what she wishes to be thought.

If another is more valued and considered than oneself, either that person is really the most meritorious, or else the delusion will in time be dissolved—the gilding will wear off with use, and the brass will be discovered. In neither case is it wise to complain. Sometimes people whose exterior is unprepossessing, and whose manners are harsh, may be unjustly disliked at first; but if their qualities within are really valuable, they will, before long, be appreciated as they deserve. We must remember, however, that there are rough pebbles as well as rough diamonds, and that bitter chestnuts have a prickly outside as well as sweet ones; so we must not fancy ourselves to be good, because we know we are disagreeable. Even when concealing a sweet and valuable kernel, these rough outsides are disadvantageous to their owners; for, though intimate associates may become aware of the good underneath, acquaintances cannot possibly guess at its existence, and a feeling of dislike may spring up which it will take years to remove. Therefore, these inconvenient disguises should be got rid of as quickly and decidedly as possible, for why should we allow our good to be evil spoken of unnecessarily? Why "mar the good we might do here" by making ourselves purposely unpleasant?

And now, I will say a few words on influence, taking it for granted that influence is a thing generally desired. Good people must wish for it when they see so much misery and wickedness around them; for how can they help desiring to possess the means of putting a stop to it ?   Bad people wish for it, that they may have plenty of companions in their wicked courses.   Only a few very selfish individuals are indifferent to it; because, not being sociable, they do not want companions, and not being good-hearted, they do not mind seeing other people make themselves miserable by their folly, or by their vices.

Thus, the great majority of the world wish for influence, and it is a legitimate object of desire, not for its own sake—not for the petty gratification of being able to persuade people to give up their will to our own, but for the noble purpose of leading them to act wisely and uprightly.

The learned Dr. Butler said, " Duty and interest are perfectly coincident, for the most part in this world, and in every instance if we take in the future."   Now, who that believes this sentence can fail to wish to lead others to believe it, and also to act up to the belief?   Let us, then, inquire what kind of persons those are who can acquire influence.   Vain people, though they so much wish to obtain it—not to exercise it, but for display—can seldom, if ever, attain it, for they seek after the opinion of the circle around them, that they may follow it, and those cannot lead who must always be following.

Self-respect and self-control, are the two great requisites in a leader, and they generally go together, as those who respect themselves will be careful not to lose their self-control ; for what is less to be respected than a human being in a state of violent anger or fear ?

Most of all, example gains influence.

Whoever persistently behaves well will be respected, and her words will come with weight.

A clever dissembler may gain respect for a time, but hypocrisy is sure to be found out before long, and, as a general rule, it deceives no one even for a moment.

Sincerity, to put it on the lowest ground, is, like honesty, the best policy, for it wins respect, even if it sometimes gives offence; but an upright life, a course of good actions, both great and small, is the real talisman for gaining influence that never fails. But this sincerity and perfect uprightness of life is not a thing easily attained. It will not be established by a simple effort of will, though such an effort will help us to attain it. In no instance is it truer that "Pride goes before a fall" than in this.

Persons who are convinced it is impossible for them to do a shabby thing, or commit a mean action, are sometimes surprised into it, or are induced to commit it, by others in whom they have confidence, without perceiving, till too late, the real character of their behaviour. This is liable to befall all inexperienced people; and women, generally, are inexperienced in anything that relates to business, so they should be specially on their guard.

The great preservative against such a fall is not to be over-confident, but to watch our own conduct carefully, and to pray God continually to keep us from everything mean and base.

No one who possesses the moral qualities requisite for obtaining influence, is so low in social station, so poor, so ignorant, as to be without it; and as God often chooses weak instruments to work with, great deeds have some-

times been done by very little men and women ; deeds
that will live in history, and have made their mark on
time.

One of such deeds was the work of John Pounds, the
cobbler, at Portsmouth. As he sat in his room in a back
street, mending shoes, he used to watch the little ragged
boys of the neighbourhood at play. He saw and heard
how ignorant they were, and how wicked they were in
danger of becoming—their parents being too poor, or too
careless to send them to school, or teach them anything
good.

At last, he was moved to take pity on them ; but what
could a poor cobbler do, a man who had to work for his
bread, and had no money to spare ? Why, he called to
them, and said he would teach any boy to read who
wished it, without charge, as he sat at his cobbling. One
or two came, and he taught them to read out of his old
Bible ; then more came, till presently his room was full.
Now and then, a starving boy would come, who had had
no food all day, and then he would give him a potato—
all he could spare.

He taught them, above all, the duty of honesty, and
many a lad who would have proved a thief, grew up
an honest labourer in consequence of his teaching.
Altogether, 500 boys passed through his school, and at
length the story got known ; people came to look at
his ragged pupils at their lessons. An artist took a
picture of the scene, engravings were made from the
picture, they were sold about the country, and one was
hung up in a little inn. It chanced to meet the eye of a
famous Scotch preacher, Dr. Guthrie ; he asked the

story, was struck with the idea, and, as he himself said, felt ashamed that he should have done so little, compared to this poor cobbler.

So he set to work, and preached that in every town schools for ragged children ought to be opened, at which no fee should be paid, no tidy clothes required, and where some coarse common food should be provided for the very famished. The scheme spread, and now, in almost every great town in England and Scotland, such schools have been established, and have proved the means of rescuing thousands of poor children from ignorance and vice. These schools are now considered very important, and are discussed in the Houses of Parliament, and able men of rank and learning dispute about the best method of conducting them, but they all arose out of the cobbler's stall at Portsmouth, and humble John Pounds was the author of the movement, and set the example which Queen, Lords, and Commons are following. Dr. Guthrie said of him, " When the day comes when honour will be done to whom honour is due, I can fancy the crowd of those whose fame poets have sung, and to whose memory monuments have been raised, dividing like a wave, and passing the great, the noble, and the mighty of the land, this poor obscure old man stepping forward, and receiving the especial notice of Him who said, ' Inasmuch as ye did it to one of the least of these, ye did it also to Me.' "

Women, also, have taken their part in the improvement of their fellow-creatures. Sarah Martin, the daughter of a working mechanic, was born in 1791, in a small village three miles from Yarmouth. Her parents dying while she was very young, she was taken care of by her grandmother.

She received her education at the village school, was afterwards apprenticed to the dress-making trade, and then earned her living by going out to sew in neighbouring families. Often, on her way to and from her work, she passed the jail, which was placed just outside the town, and always thought with pity of the poor creatures within, and even when as young as nineteen, began to wish she could be admitted to read the Scriptures to them, and to help them to be less wicked and miserable.

Some nine years afterwards, the opportunity for doing so occurred. A woman from her neighbourhood was committed to prison for child-murder ; Sarah went to see her, and thus relates the interview :—

" When I told her the motive of my visit, of her guilt, and her need of God's mercy, she burst into tears and thanked me."

Her reception proved her fitness for the task : she found she possessed power to move the prisoners, and visited them as often as she could find time ; she taught the women to sew and knit, and the men to make boys' caps, for, till then, they had been quite idle, and all who wished to learn, she taught to read.

Old men, who had grown grey in crime, might be seen reading out of children's primers. Violent and depraved women grew submissive and gentle under her influence, and would learn verses of the Scripture by heart at her bidding, and all these operations, be it observed, were carried on with no authority save what was derived from the teacher's own innate force of character. But, successful as were her prison ministrations, she feared to be obliged to give them up, for they occupied almost all her time, and she had her own livelihood to earn.

Some inhabitants of the town, who respected her exertions, and saw how much good she had effected, made a representation to the Government in behalf of the prisoners, and in consequence Sarah was given a small salary of £15 or £20 a-year, just enough to live on, and so she went on with the good work she had begun, and added other good works to it, teaching in the evenings at a large school for factory girls, and visiting the sick in the workhouse.

Thus she lived for many years, and so happy was she made by her useful life, that persons passing her lodging at night, often heard her singing merrily to herself, as she was preparing for rest. She died in 1842, aged fifty-two years. After her death, the journal she had kept in reference to the prisoners, and some other records of hers, were presented to the public library at Yarmouth, and are there preserved. Her life has often been written in detail; but the best memorial in her honour is the improvement in the jail, which has never fallen back into its old neglected state. So her usefulness extends beyond the grave, and her work still lives, though she has gone to her rest.

A still greater effect for good was produced by another woman, in a yet humbler sphere of life, and by one who could neither read nor write.

Elizabeth Freeman, or "Mum Bett," as she was generally called, from her silent habits, was born about

1742, in the neighbourhood of New York, in America. She was a negress, her parents being natives of Africa, who were kidnapped and carried off to be sold as slaves. When ten years old, she and a younger sister were sold away from their father and mother by their owner, to a gentleman who lived in the State of Massachusetts, in which it was then lawful to keep slaves. Here she lived for many years, till one day the lady of the house, in a fit of passion, struck at the younger sister with a heated kitchen shovel. Mum Bett interposed her arm, and received the blow, the scar of which she bore to the day of her death. She resented the outrage and left the house.

But Mum Bett was only a slave, and her master appealed to the law to have her sent back. She, on her part, called on Mr. Sedgwick, a kind and clever lawyer, and asked him if she could not claim her liberty under the law. He inquired what could put such an idea into her head? She replied, that the Bill of Rights declared all mankind to be born free, and that, as she was not a dumb beast, she must be free also. When asked how she had learnt to reason thus, she answered, " By biding still and minding things; " for it was a favourite theory of hers, that people might learn much by keeping still, and minding what went on around them. On being requested to explain herself further, she said, that when waiting at table, she had heard gentlemen talking over the Bill of Rights, and the new Constitution of Massachusetts, and had thus learnt that all people were declared to be born free and equal, and so resolved she would try whether she did not come in among them.

The framers of this law had never intended to include
black men; they had only meant to declare that white
people were, by nature, free; but as they had said
nothing about negroes, and had not excluded them, it
gave a chance of obtaining freedom, which Mum Bett
had been acute enough to perceive.   Mr. Sedgwick
undertook her cause, and won it.   She obtained her
freedom, and a sum of money as compensation for her
services since she was twenty-one.   "What shall I do
with all this money of yours?" inquired Mr. Sedgwick.
"Fee all the lawyers well; pay 'em handsomely," said
she, "and keep the rest till I ask for it."

This was wise and generous, for by paying the lawyers
handsomely, she would encourage them to help any other
slave in the same position.   A selfish person would have
paid no more than she was compelled, and kept as much
as she could for herself; but Mum Bett thought of the
rights and interests of others, as well as of her own.
Her example was followed by many slaves, and from the
day of her emancipation, more and more negroes claimed
and received their liberty under the Bill of Rights, till at
last, slavery was abolished in the State of Massachusetts.
Thus, a poor ignorant woman was a chief instrument in
obtaining freedom for hundreds, perhaps thousands, of
her fellow-creatures.   By her courage and sense, she
abolished more misery and created more happiness than
ten thousand pounds spent in charity could have done.*

---

* This story is from "Retrospect of Western Travel," by Harriet
Martineau, page 104.

These examples have been chosen to show how much good may be effected by persons possessed of no external advantages whatever, and with no help but that afforded by their own sense and good feeling ; but persons possessed of higher qualifications and advantages have it in their power to effect yet more.   Mrs. Fry, being wealthy, well-educated, and belonging to an influential family, did on a large scale what Sarah Martin did on a small one, and reformed not one jail, but many.

Mrs. Chisholm, in our own time, has been the means of giving happiness to hundreds.   Feeling acutely for the sufferings which women often have to undergo to earn their bread in their restricted field of labour at home, she raised money by subscription to hire a ship to take some away to the colonies, and when she had collected a shipload, she went out with them to make sure that they were well treated on the voyage.   When they had arrived, after as many servants had been engaged as were wanted in the towns, she hired waggons for the rest and took them into the country, dropping a girl or two at every farmhouse, the country people being sadly in want of servants, till at last all had got situations, and she returned with an empty train of waggons.   This voyage and journey she repeated many times, so that numbers of poor women are now in Australia, earning good wages, or perhaps comfortably married, who would otherwise have been struggling for bread in England. Yet Mrs. Chisholm had not many advantages.   She was never rich, and possessed no influence but what she won by her kind heart and a hand ever ready to help.   Her health having failed, she has given up her voyages, and having become a widow she is now living in Australia, where she has to support herself, and where she must often meet some of her former emigrants, who, it is to be hoped, show her the gratitude she deserves.

It is sometimes said that though women are often very charitable to individuals, yet they are too narrow-minded to devise or carry out a scheme to help whole classes of sufferers, because they feel pity only for misery that is actually before their eyes, and have no compassion for that which is out of their sight, even though they know it to exist.   A poet, and a female poet too, says,—

> "None of these things
> Can woman understand. You generalize—
> Oh, nothing! not even grief.   *   *   *
> *   *   *   A red-hair'd child
> Sick in a fever, if you touch him once,
> Though but so little as with a finger-tip,
> Will set you weeping; but a million sick—
> You could as soon weep for the rule of three
> Or compound fractions. Therefore this same world
> By you uncomprehended, must remain
> By you uninfluenced. Women as you are—
> Mere women—personal and passionate."

Now, whether this be true or not as a rule, there are certainly many exceptions. Neither Mrs. Fry nor Sarah Martin had any acquaintance with the prisoners before they went among them, nor could Mrs. Chisholm have had a personal interest in each of the many hundred girls she took out with her; she pitied them as a class, and helped them as a class.

I am inclined, therefore, to think the poet's accusation untrue, and that the reason why women so seldom succeed in doing good on a large scale proceeds more from ignorance of business than from want of the power of generalizing. Still the fact remains true, that persons, who can form a plan for helping a class, do much more good than those who give away shillings and sixpences in assisting individuals; and of all plans for helping people, those are the best which enable them to help themselves.

I am far, however, from wishing to depreciate almsgiving, as there are many cases of distress in which such help is much wanted. To provide persons with employment and other means of self-help is to cure the disease of misery. Almsgiving is a palliative only, but the cure is of such slow process, that often the patient would die before it could take effect if it were not for the palliative.

Still, we must never fancy that almsgiving can cure misery, for as it is of the nature of moral evil it can only be cured by enabling those afflicted with it to fight against and cast it off for themselves. The best plan, however, is to guard against its approaches while it is still far off, by diligent and vigorous " self-help."

At this moment a plan for helping working women to help themselves is much wanted. It is a plan that can only be carried out by working women, and I cannot help hoping that, if I succeed in showing how great its advantages would be, some of my readers may have sufficient knowledge of business to put it into execution.

By a working woman I mean a woman who maintains
herself by her own honourable industry, to whatever
sphere of life she may belong, and the plan to which
I allude is that of forming benefit societies for working
women.

CHAPTER VII.

Benefit Societies for Women.

"Bear ye one another's burdens, and so fulfil the law of Christ."
Gal. vi. 2.

BENEFIT societies for men have existed for many years in all parts of the country, but societies for women are less numerous and seem to be chiefly confined to the northern and western counties, though here and there one is to be found in other districts.

Benefit societies are said to be French inventions, and to have been imported into this country by the persecuted protestants, who took refuge here after the revocation of the edict of Nantes. There are a great number now in France for men and several for women.

M. Simon, a French writer of celebrity, gives an account of these clubs for women in a book called "L'ouvriere," ("The Working Woman") as follows:—

"Although the number of members in all France does not exceed twelve thousand, the result may be considered conclusive. The societies have been well managed, the meetings have passed quietly, and the receipts have exceeded the expenses,—an indispensable condition of success. The number of honorary members is less

considerable in the societies for women than in those for
men, a circumstance much to be regretted, but which
will probably disappear when the principles of these
female societies are better known and more fully appreciated.   Ladies can in no way do more good at a less
expense than by assisting these institutions, which serve
as protections to the health and morals of young girls
and single women.   A poor woman who belongs to no
society does not send for the doctor till the illness has
become serious.   That alone is an injury, not only to
the sick person, but also to the public health.   Societies
would put an end to that ; they would also suppress
the most frequent cause of want, that is, being out of
work from illness, and they would supply the place of
a family to single women.   Now, the causes of women
falling into bad courses, are first want, and secondly
loneliness."

M. Simon further tells us, that the first society for
women was founded at Grenoble in the year 1822 ; and
as there were 140 when he wrote in 1861, they must
have spread pretty rapidly.   If similar societies were
spreading with equal rapidity in England, women would
have cause to congratulate themselves, for there is not
a class of " breadwinners " to whom these societies would
not prove a comfort and support.   From the highly
educated and well-salaried governess,* down to the
poorest maid-servant† or agricultural labourer—all would

* A sick fund might perhaps be added to that admirable Charity,
the Governesses' Benevolent Institution.

† A benefit club might be established with advantage in connexion
with every Register office for servants, the servants paying contributions

feel the benefit of these institutions. At present, when illness comes, there follows loss of employment, a rapid consumption of scanty savings, then the pain of falling a heavy burden on family or friends, and finally, in some cases, an appeal to private charity, or perhaps a bed in the workhouse infirmary.

I have said enough to show how desirable it is that benefit societies for women should be established in all parts of the country, and now proceed to treat of the practical work of establishing them; but on this point I speak with diffidence, for not having had a share in establishing one myself, I cannot give my own experience, but can only quote from books or the experience of others. Still, the information I can give may be of use.

Benefit societies may be established under very different rules, but some principles apply to all alike. A society would hardly be safe which contained less than fifty members. From seventy to two hundred seems to be about the best number, as that is enough for security without becoming difficult to manage. The average number in Frenchwomen's clubs is eighty-five. In all cases members must subscribe for at least three months before receiving any benefits, and it is usually better to require a subscription of six months. The reason is that if there was no fund in hand to begin with, a sudden epidemic might cause bankruptcy at once. The sick

and receiving sick allowances in proportion to their wages. Women of education could not confer a greater boon on their poorer sisters than by taking the necessary trouble for the establishment and management of these societies. Unfortunately, ladies, though often generous of their money, are seldom inclined to take trouble.

allowance should also, without exception, be very considerably smaller than the salary or wages earned while in health.   If it is the same, or nearly the same, idle members will be tempted to pretend they are ill in order to obtain it ; or if they do not positively resort to deception, will be inclined to fancy themselves in worse health than they really are.   Thus, the educated worker who earns a pound a week ought to receive no more than fifteen shillings as sick allowance, and on the same principle the field labourer who earns only five or six shillings a week should receive no more than four shillings.

Another rule should be observed—*i.e*, the woman whose work is partly domestic, partly away from home, should not receive the *full* sick allowance when too ill to do her out-door work, but not too ill to do her home work.   She should then receive the half allowance only.   Thus, if a person who receives her board and lodging in return for acting as companion or housekeeper to some relation or friend, and earns money besides by daily teaching or some other occupation away from home, should become too ill to teach, but is still able to continue to act as companion or housekeeper, she should receive the half allowance ; but if too ill to keep her situation as house-keeper or companion, she should receive the whole allowance.

Also, if the wife of a day labourer, whose usual occupation is taking care of her children, but who sometimes goes out to work, should fall ill and be unable to go out to work, but is still able to perform her domestic work, she should receive the half allowance, but if too ill to do her household work she should receive the whole allowance. Experience has shewn the necessity of this rule, for when the full allowance is given, women, whose occupations are partly domestic, have proved themselves apt to give way to the slightest indisposition, and thus subject the club to much unnecessary expense.

The chief consideration on starting a club is, what amount of monthly contribution is required to obtain the requisite sick allowance. The following table, which has received the approbation of the eminent actuary, Mr. S. Brown, of the Guardian Assurance Office, will assist in deciding this point. Benefits and contributions to cease at sixty years of age.

A monthly contribution of

Class	s.	d.		£	s.	
1	2	2	will secure	1	0	per week for 26 weeks
2	1	7	,,	0	15	,, ,,
3	1	1	,,	0	10	,, ,,
4	0	8	,,	0	6	,, ,,
5	0	5	,,	0	4	,, ,,

If the illness lasts longer than twenty-six weeks, the allowance must be reduced to one-half; if it lasts longer than fifty-two weeks, it must be reduced to one quarter, which will be continued for the remainder of the illness.

Extra yearly payments must also be made according to age, as follows,

Class	Under 20	20 to 25		25 to 30		30 to 35		35 and upwards	
		s.	d.	s.	d.	s.	d.	s.	d.
1	Nothing	2	0	4	0	6	0	8	0
2	,,	1	6	3	0	4	6	6	0
3	,,	1	0	2	0	3	0	4	0
4	,,	0	8	1	4	2	0	2	8
5	,,	0	5	0	10	1	3	1	8

If extra yearly payments are found inconvenient and a uniform system, without distinction of age, is preferred, it appears obvious that the yearly payment made between thirty and thirty-five should be divided into twelve parts, and one part added to each monthly payment. Thus the monthly contribution of 2s. 2d. to secure £1 a week, would be increased to 2s. 8d. and so on. This, however, is only my own suggestion; Mr. Brown has not sanctioned it. It should be observed that the sick allowance is calculated to cease at sixty; if it is desired to continue it for life, higher monthly contributions must be made.

I do not know how much higher the contribution ought to be; an actuary must be applied to for that information. If the monthly contributions are thought too high, they may be lowered by reducing the number of weeks during which the full sick allowance is given, and granting it for only twelve or sixteen weeks. I cannot undertake to say in what proportion it ought to be reduced.

The government of the club must depend on the amount of education and intelligence to be found among its members.

Clubs for the educated classes may be entirely self-governed, those for the uneducated would require the supervision of honorary members; but some share of the management should always remain with the ordinary members, or public spirit will be liable to diminish among them. The best way of obtaining a good constitution, would be to read over the rules of two or three successful well-managed clubs, whether for men or women, and adopt the plan which appears the best, with such modifications as may be required. Some rules, however, apply to all.

Great care should be taken to secure the club fund from dishonesty. To effect this, the Secretary should be required to give security, and no larger sum should be allowed to remain in her hands than that for which she has given security. Anything more than this should be paid into the Post Office Savings Bank, out of which it should be impossible for anyone to draw any money without the signature of three trustees, who must be persons of great respectability.

Every club to be successful must accumulate a large fund during the first years of its formation, for the reason that young people are less liable to illness than old ones, therefore, while the members are young, they pay more than is required for their immediate wants; this money accumulates, and the interest arising from it will be found necessary when the members are old. The amount of illness to be expected in a woman's club, and its gradual increase as old age approaches is shewn in the following table from the government returns.*

The average amount of sickness per annum to each person, expressed in days.

Age.	Females.
20	8.22
25	8.03
30	9.00
35	10.28
40	10.09
45	11.27
50	13.15
60	20.66

* Mr. Glenfindlaison's report. 1853.   Page xxvii.

H

On account of this increase in illness as life advances, it is necessary to prevent old persons from joining the club, for if the club has not made a profit upon them while young, it cannot afford a loss upon them when old.

In order to encourage persons to join while young, a sliding scale of entrance fees ought to be established according to age—very low—or nothing for members under twenty-five, more considerable between that age and thirty, very high between thirty and thirty-five, and almost prohibitory between thirty-five and forty. After forty no one ought to be admitted, and persons known to have chronic bad health must be excluded also.

When a club has not many honorary members, but is intended to be really self-supporting, this rule must be strictly adhered to, or bankruptcy will ensue.

Various modes exist in the different clubs by which sick members apply for the allowance, and though this seems unimportant, experience shows that much depends on it.

It is not unusual for the sick member to send for the club doctor, and ask him for a certificate of illness, and this certificate being sent to the secretary, procures a week's allowance.

Another plan is for the sick member to send for an officer of the society, called a steward or visitor, who, if she thinks fit, gives an order for the doctor, and another for the week's allowance. If the member is refused the allowance, and thinks herself aggrieved, she may complain to the committee which meets every month. The first plan is the simplest, and avoids disputes; but in some instances it appears to lead to extravagance, as the doctor, if an easy-going good-natured man, will give certificates too readily without a sufficiently careful scrutiny. The steward, having the interests of the club at heart, is usually stricter. The accounts of two clubs are now before me, and in that where the doctor's certificate secures the allowance, the amount of illness paid for has been for some years almost double that of the club, where the allowance is given on the order of the steward. When the former plan is followed, the doctor should at least be appointed by the managing committee, not elected by the members, and a very careful doctor selected.

When the members of a club are very poor, fortnightly contributions are more easily paid than monthly ones. If a member does not pay her contribution for three months, she should be considered to have withdrawn, and be entitled to no sick allowance unless she pays up all at once.

In clubs for wealthier persons, the contributions might be payable quarterly, and a member not be considered as withdrawn under six months' cessation of subscription.

In all cases members who have removed to a distance, should be required to pay only once in three months, and should receive their allowance on the certificate of the doctor who attends them, together with that of the clergyman of the parish, or some respectable householder.

The expense of a club doctor is usually three shillings a year for each member, for which he is bound to furnish medicines gratis. This necessitates an extra expense of threepence per monthly contribution. Some clubs do not employ a doctor, but when it can be afforded, the attendance of a doctor is doubtless a great benefit.

In many cases a sum towards funeral expenses is also provided by the club. The monthly contribution of one penny secures one pound five shillings for the funeral.

The expenses of managing the club vary according to the wealth of the members. A penny a month for each member seems to be the minimum ; and in some clubs the honorary members undertake to pay for this part of the concern. Threepence a month per member is a very usual charge for expenses when paid by the ordinary members. The salary of the secretary varies from two pounds a year to twenty-five pounds, according to the wealth of the club.

The visitors are frequently paid, but sometimes the members of the club take the office in turn without pay. It would probably be better to pay them when the club can afford it. I think I have now touched on the chief points, which concern the welfare of a benefit club. There is every reason to believe that women's clubs, when founded on good principles, are perfectly successful. One was established by a clergyman in the agricultural village of Hawkshead, on the borders of Westmoreland and Lancashire, in 1798, and is still flourishing with one hundred and seventy members, and a fund of above £900. This club gives the sick allowance for life, but after sixty the half allowance only is given. The members are chiefly labourers' wives and maid-servants ; and only three pounds a year is received from honorary members.

Benefit societies would be of much service to dress-makers, and shopwomen in towns. One which was started in 1863 in London, for female telegraph clerks, gives good promise of success.

No fear need be entertained that the tables here given are not high enough, they are at least higher than those of the successful club at Hawkshead. They are amply sufficient unless deception is practised with regard to illness, and if deception becomes customary among the members of a club, it is impossible to say how high the tables ought to be to allow for it.

It is stated, I regret to say, that much feigned illness is to be found among women in clubs. I believe that this occurs, not in women's clubs, but in mixed clubs for men and women, and when it is the case it will be also found, I think, that women are not admitted to a full share of the management of the society or of the offices belonging to it. This diminishes their interest in the institution, and causes them to consider it a mere instrument for obtaining money. Their public spirit being checked, a selfish one springs up in its place. This exclusion from office does not justify the dishonest conduct of the female members, but it accounts for and in some degree excuses it. The first departure from equity comes at least from the side of the male members. Female members should remember, however, that wrong doing ought not to be counteracted by more wrong doing. If an injustice cannot be resisted, it should be endured, and not revenged by another act of injustice committed with subtlety. The women who have thus acted have degraded themselves, and given their whole sex a bad character for trustworthiness and honourable dealing.

Whenever men or women are in the same club, the

women ought, in justice, to be eligible for the committee of management, and a certain number, according to the proportion of women in the club, ought to be placed upon it; if this is not done, the men may feel sure that the public spirit of the women with regard to the interests of the club will be less keen than their own. And this is not the result of any feminine peculiarity, but is a part of human nature. If the brown-haired men in a club were to decide that the black-haired men should hold no offices in it, the public spirit of the black-haired men would soon be found to decline. Above all, women visitors for the sick should be instituted (unless a doctor is employed to give certificates) whenever women are admitted into the club, and if the male visitor is paid, the female visitor should be paid also. If any woman was inclined to feign illness, she would find it more difficult to deceive one of her own sex than a man.

In a mixed club, where the men subscribe for a high rate of sick allowance, the sick allowance of the women should be less than half that of the men, as the wages of women are (at least in agricultural districts) less than half those of men. Also, as women have a greater share of illness than men, they ought to pay rather more in proportion.* Thus, if a man paid 1s. 2d. a month to secure a sick allowance of 10s. a week until sixty-five, a woman ought to pay 7d. (half) a month to secure 4s. 6d. a week sick allowance, somewhat less than half.

* The following table from the government returns shows the amount of illness among men and women. Mr. Glenfindlaison's Report, pp. 22 and 55. Average amount of sickness per annum to each person expressed in days.

The rule should also be observed, that women whose work is partly domestic, partly out of doors, are to receive only the half allowance unless too ill to do their domestic work.

Under just regulations men and women might join together in a club with success; but as it would be troublesome and difficult to secure just regulations, especially that of admitting the women to an equal share of the honours and offices, it is probably better to form separate clubs for each sex.

I believe that if these societies for mutual help were generally established among women, they would confer

Age.	Men engaged in light labour	Men engaged in heavy labr.	Females.
20	6.42	7.10	8.58
25	5.97	7.34	8.03
30	5.98	7.57	9.00
35	6.13	7.92	10.28
40	7.16	9.10	10.09
45	7.94	10.58	11.27
50	10.40	12.48	13.15
60	16.15	21.42	20.66
70	40.86	46.65	32.81
80	90.96	104.25	55.97
	197.97	234.41	179.84

This gives women a less proportion of illness than men, and no doubt there is less illness among women in clubs which continue to give the sick allowance for *life*. But as a general rule, clubs in England cease at 60 or 65, which leaves a greater proportion of illness to women. If the tables ended at 60, the number of days' sickness would be, light labour, 66.15; heavy labour, 85.51; women, 91.6. Agricultural labourers are included under the head of heavy labour. Women have about one-sixteenth more illness than men engaged in heavy labour. The difference between women and men engaged in light labour is far greater.

inestimable benefits upon them, especially on single women; for not only the help in sickness would be of great value, but the companionship and interest of such a society would cheer their lives, and give them a pleasant interest.* The employments of women are frequently necessarily tedious and frivolous; this tedium and frivolity they often feel painfully, and it produces in them a kind of self-contempt. This is not observable in men. A stout young fellow will sell ribbons for years, and keep a high opinion of himself all the while; and the reason of this difference I believe to be that he is something more than a ribbon-seller when out of the shop. Perhaps he is a rifle volunteer, or a good hand at cricket, or he belongs to a debating club, or has some office in a benefit society, or possesses some other pursuit or avocation, in which he fills a position of importance, and this knowledge keeps up his self-respect. If in the day he is a mere drudge, when evening comes he is somebody: thus he does not suffer from the humiliation of his position. But with working women the case is different;

---

* Benefit clubs ought not to attempt to give allowances to persons out of work, as so to do would encourage the idle or fastidious to decline situations. It is true that very industrious women are often out of place from no fault of their own, even when in health; but as it would be impossible to distinguish between those who could not get work and those who did not choose to take it, the attempt should be avoided altogether, as it would end in the idle being maintained by the industrious. It is a proper measure of precaution to send a copy of the Rules, before they are printed, to John Tidd Pratt Esq., Registrar of Benefit Societies, 28, Abingdon Street, Westminster; as Mr. Tidd Pratt would point out any illegality in the rules, and in some cases has given many useful directions.

their position never changes, they are seldom important, seldom looked up to with respect, and so their own self-respect dies out, and they learn self-contempt.

Mr. Trollope, in his book on America,* speaks of the painfully humble look and manner of English girls of the middle and lower ranks. This humility is a misfortune, not a virtue; it springs from unhappiness, and it leads to misery; for women who have this feeling acquiesce in their own wretchedness, and seem to think that any kind of bad treatment is good enough for such poor creatures as they are. They will not struggle against injustice or misfortune, but yield to it at once, as if they knew it was their fate to be miserable.

I am convinced, therefore, that one indispensable step towards improving the position of women must be, to call forth their own self-respect and to raise them in their own estimation, and I see no way of doing it effectually except by means of these societies. The woman who is a member of one of these useful self-supporting institutions, and who has a voice and a vote at the half-yearly meetings for the direction of its affairs, cannot fail to feel some respect for herself. When she belongs to an important community, a sense of her own importance will grow up in her mind, and a portion of its dignity will be reflected upon herself. If she is an officer in the society, her sense of dignity and usefulness will be proportionally increased; and if her life is solitary, the companionship and the friendship which will spring out of the society, will cheer her loneliness. Thus she will be encouraged

* Vol. I. page 315.

and cheered to make a struggle against fortune, and to strive to maintain herself in a respectable position. For as M. de Tocqueville says, "The humblest individual who is called upon to co-operate in the government of society acquires a certain degree of self-respect." Other good and great qualities in her will also be drawn out, and anything of meanness or pettiness be repressed. Mr. Stuart Mill so well describes the effect on the human mind of joining in any public business, that I will quote his words:—"The private money-getting occupation of almost every one is more or less mechanical routine; it brings but few of his faculties into action, while its exclusive pursuit tends to fasten his attention and interest exclusively on himself, and upon his family as an appendage to himself, making him indifferent to the public, to the more generous objects and the nobler interests, and in his inordinate regard for his personal comforts, selfish and cowardly. Balance these tendencies by contrary ones, give him something to do for the public, whether as a vestryman, a juror, or an elector, and in his degree his ideas and feelings are taken out of their narrow circle. He becomes acquainted with more varied business, and a larger range of considerations. He is made to feel that besides the interests which separate him from his fellow-citizens, he has interests which connect him with them, that not only the common weal is his weal, but that it partly depends upon his exertions."*

Now, this description relates to human nature, and

* Dissertations and Discussions, by J. S. Mill. Vol. II., p. 24.

is, therefore, as true of women as of men, and women as well as men are morally improved by engaging in any work which regards the public good. Women of wealth obtain this practical moral education by engaging in charitable undertakings, but women who have no money to spare can do nothing for the public good: thus they grow narrow in their ideas; if they are married, they take interest in little save their families; if they are single, they take interest in little but themselves. Those who are by nature hard grow selfish, and if they are not naturally hard but generous, they then become desponding, through feeling the littleness of a life lived only for self, and so end by despising their position and themselves.

Thus, friendly societies would bestow on our working women important indirect benefits, besides the immediate advantages of support in sickness and medical advice. Yet, in the establishment of these institutions, much caution should be observed, especially in the choice of officers, otherwise they may do harm instead of good. I would strongly recommend any persons who may think of starting a society of this sort, not on any account to employ men as secretaries or treasurers, as their superior knowledge of business would enable them, if dishonestly inclined, to defraud the subscribers without danger of discovery. An exception might perhaps be made in favour of some man of established good character. I am only speaking of a general rule, but it is a rule that should not be departed from save in some very exceptional case. There would,

however, be no objection, but rather the contrary, to
the employment of men among the competent persons
engaged to overlook the accounts at the end of the
half-year.

In the management of these associations perfect
integrity must be observed, not only with regard to
money—that is self-evident—but on other points.
There should be no unfair grasping after power or credit,
no packing of committees, no carrying of measures by
surprise. In men's associations these evils are not
uncommon, but men have such habits of business, so
much knowledge of the world, that though business is
impeded and success diminished by intrigues, it is still
possible to go on with the undertaking. With women
this would not be the case. Any attempt at unfairness
would prove the ruin of the enterprise ; for a want of fair
dealing once perceived, discouragement would creep in,
as no one would know how to stop it, or how far it might
go. All manœuvres, even for objects good in themselves, should be strictly avoided, as an undertaking
would be less injured by the honest carrying of a bad
measure, than by the dishonest carrying of a good one.
The bad measure may in time be discovered to be a
mistake and be rescinded, or the evil effects from it not
prove as great as was expected ; but the discovery of
unfairness among colleagues and fellow-workers would
spread a fatal distrust and sense of insecurity amongst
all concerned.

Bad means cannot serve a good cause ; and as the
cause of the improvement of the position of women,

the most numerous but least powerful half of the human race, is a good and sacred cause—perhaps the best and most sacred of all causes—it can only be served by good and honourable means, by uprightness, truthfulness, and open dealing.

CHAPTER VIII.

𝕳𝖊𝖆𝖉-𝖂𝖔𝖗𝖐 𝖆𝖓𝖉 𝕳𝖊𝖆𝖗𝖙-𝖂𝖔𝖗𝖐.

Evil is wrought by want of thought
As well as want of heart.—*Hood.*

"Pray, Mr. Opie, may I ask what you mix your colours
with?" said a brisk, dilettante student to the great
painter. "With *brains!* sir," was the gruff reply,
and the right one. It did not give much of what we
should call information; it did not explain the principles
and rules of art: but if the inquirer possessed the com-
modity referred to, it would awaken him, it would set
him a-going, a-thinking, and a-painting to good purpose.
If he had not the wherewithal, as was likely enough, the
less he had to do with colours and their mixture the
better.

Again, Etty was appointed teacher of the Royal
Academy, when, having been preceded by a clever,
talkative, scientific expounder of æsthetics, who delighted
to tell young men *how* everything was done, how to copy
this, how to express that, a student came up to the new
master, "How should I do this, sir?" "Suppose you
try." Another: "What does this mean, Mr. Etty?"

"Suppose you look." "But I have looked." "Suppose you look again." And they did try, and they did look, and looked again, and saw and achieved what they never would have seen and done, had the how and the what been told them and done for them. These anecdotes from "Horæ Subsecivæ," by Dr. John Brown, are intended to show that it is impossible to teach people to do anything well unless they will take the trouble of trying to learn,— and not of trying with the hand only, which people are often willing to do, but with their heads also, and using their brains to think and reason about the matter taught. A schoolmaster is reported to have said to his scholars, "Think wrong, if you like, but think for yourselves :" knowing very well that if they once learnt to think at all they would think to good purpose some day. People who learn with their hands only, and do not use their heads too, may become tolerable third-rate workmen, but will never rise to the first rank. It is said by a gentleman who ought to know, that young women are very idle in this respect, and that they avoid thinking and using their brains as much as possible ; and to this he attributes the fact that few women have risen to the highest eminence in those professions and employments which are open to them.

The gentleman who speaks thus is Mr. Hutton, Professor of Mathematics in the Ladies' College, Bedford Square.

Mr. Hutton mentions as instances of women who have risen to the highest ranks in their professions—art and literature, Rosa Bonheur, and the author of "Adam Bede." We have seen how thorough was Rosa Bonheur's

art education, and how she put her whole heart in her
work, and used not her fingers only but every faculty she
possessed to attain to excellence.   The author of "Adam
Bede" is well known to be a very learned person, and to
have tackled the toughest and most profound regions of
thought; and to these reasoning habits, and to the power
of mind educed by such studies, which enabled her to
understand and perceive the depth and breadth of every
subject she writes on, not its superficial aspect only, Mr.
Hutton attributes her success as an author.   "Is it a mere
accident," he says, "that she can venture with so much
success where her competitors and peers [other female
writers] dare not tread ?   Or is it not surely that that
power of generalizing and passing beyond the sphere of
individual observation, which is generally reserved for
men, has been conquered by her in consequence of the
bracing influence of her masculine studies?"   The
author of "Adam Bede" herself seems to be of opinion
that teaching is of little use unless the learners will
"try," and "look," and "think" for themselves, as is
shown in an amusing scene in one of her novels between
an old schoolmaster and the young men in his night
school.

   "After the reading class, two youths, between sixteen
and nineteen, came up with an imaginary bill of parcels,
which they had been writing out on their slates, and
were now required to calculate "off-hand,"—a test
which they stood with such imperfect success, that Bartle
Massey (the schoolmaster) whose eyes had been glaring
at them for some minutes through his spectacles, at
length burst out, in a high-pitched tone, "Now, you

see, you don't do this thing a bit better than you did a
fortnight ago, and I'll tell you the reason. You want to
learn accounts, that's well and good; but you think all
you need do to learn accounts, is to come to me and to
do sums for an hour or so, two or three times a-week;
and no sooner do you get your caps on and turn out of
doors again, than you sweep the whole thing clean out of
your mind; you go whistling about, and take no more care
what you're thinking of than if your heads were gutters
for any rubbish to swill through that happened to be in
the way, and if you get a good notion in 'em, it's pretty
soon washed out again. You think knowledge is to
be got cheap—you'll come and pay Bartle Massy
sixpence a-week, and he'll make you clever at figures
without your taking trouble; but knowledge isn't to be
got by paying sixpence, let me tell you; if you're to
know figures, you must turn 'em over in your heads,
and keep your thoughts fixed on 'em. There's nothing
you can't turn into a sum, for there's nothing but what's
got a number in it—even a fool. You may say to yourself, ' I am one fool, and Jack's another; if my fool's
head weighed four pounds, and Jack's three pounds
three ounces and three quarters, how many pennyweights
heavier would my head be than Jack's?' A man that
had got his heart in learning figures, would make sums
for himself and work them in his head: when he sat
shoemaking he'd count his stitches by fives, and then put
a price on the stitches, say half a farthing, and then see
how much money he could earn in an hour, and then ask
himself how much money he'd get in a day at that rate
and then how much ten workmen would get working

three, or twenty, or a hundred years at that rate, and all
the while his needle would be going just as fast as if he
left his head empty for the devil to dance in. But the
long and short of it is, I'll have nobody in my night
school that doesn't strive to learn what he comes to
learn, as hard as if he was trying to get out of a dark
hole into broad daylight. I'll send no man away because
he's stupid; if Billy Taft, the idiot, wanted to learn
anything I'd not refuse to teach him; but I'll not throw
away good knowledge on people who think they can get
it by the sixpennyworth, and carry it away with 'em as
they would an ounce of snuff. So never come to me
again, if you can't show that you've been working with
your heads, instead of thinking you can pay mine to
work for you. That's the last word I've got to say to
you."

This advice is most admirable, and is just as applicable
to women as to men, for neither one nor the other can
learn anything well unless they think of it out of the
hours of study. It seems certain that a want of education
is at the bottom of much of the difficulty which women
experience in finding employment, for it is evident that
unintelligent people cannot be employed in situations
where intelligence is required, and if people are ill taught,
they are likely enough to remain unintelligent; but this
is only a reason the more why young women should try
to teach themselves, as the less help they receive from
others, the more they must try to help themselves.
There is an error into which a girl who is naturally
clever, or who by chance has received a tolerable education,
is very apt to fall, viz., she compares herself to other

girls, and finding herself superior to them, fancies that she is a superior person, and becomes conceited, instead of remembering that it is very easy to be superior to other girls, and yet to be inferior to well-educated persons. It is with these she should compare herself, with her own brothers, for instance, and if she finds herself inferior to them in knowledge, powers of calculation, or general intelligence, she may feel sure that she will not be considered clever in business, or become a useful member of society.

I do not deny that it is hard that they who naturally suffer from inferiority in physical strength, should be compelled to suffer from another and artificial inferiority also. It is hard ; but nothing was ever yet gained by grumbling, and the only sensible thing to be done is for women to set to work and try to improve themselves as much as they can. And they should remember that no one, no employer at least, will ever make the least allowance for the difficulties an assistant may have laboured under as to education. Ne deficiencies will be excused on that score. If a clerk or saleswoman is equal to her business, she will be kept, if not, she will be dismissed without the least regard to her want of opportunity for learning ; so young women had better try and learn for themselves, and make the most of any little teaching they may get at private schools, for they will be punished for the deficiencies of their education, unless by extra exertion they can contrive to make up for it. Every woman of the middle classes cannot marry, and even those who do, will have probably to maintain themselves for some years first, and unless they can manage to attain to the average rate of intelligence possessed by persons who have been better educated than they are, they will not find it easy, perhaps not possible, to earn a livelihood. The task is a hard one, but it is necessary to be done, and by diligence much may be effected. They have probably learnt writing and a little arithmetic at school; these are the two great essentials, and they may improve themselves in these at home by self-teaching. They should try to develope their thinking powers, and should remember that in everything there is a reason and a principle, even in the smallest actions, and that people who perceive that principle and understand that reason will succeed, and that those who fail to see and understand will not succeed.

The rules of art apply as much to the trimming of a dress as to the painting of a picture. Those who understand them will be able to paint saleable pictures and trim saleable gowns pretty nearly to a certainty, while those who do not understand the rules, but paint and trim from their own tastes only, will often fail.* The same principle applies even to the making of a pudding; if a person knows the exact proportion of the materials, she can always make a good one, but if she does it by guesswork, a *good deal* of flour, a *little* sugar, *some* milk, and boils it a *good while*, instead of a certain number of minutes or hours, it will very often prove a failure. There is also a principle of reason in cutting out the shape of a gown. The person who knows this

* An English painter has set up at Paris as dressmaker. His knowledge of art enables him to decorate gowns more tastefully than any of the regular milliners, and he is making his fortune.

principle will always be able to make a good fit, those who do not will only make a good one now and then by chance. A tailor will take a measure for a riding habit with a piece of tape in five minutes, or you may take your own measure and send it him, and the habit will fit perfectly ; and a French dressmaker can do the same if required, because the tailor and the Frenchwoman are both to a certain degree educated, and have had their reason developed. The poor uneducated unreasoning Englishwoman spends a quarter of an hour and a box full of pins in fitting on an elaborate calico shape, and after all the gown probably does not fit. The consequence is that ladies employ tailors to make their habits, and often Frenchwomen to make their gowns. Thus, in everything, in the humblest as in the highest professions, intelligence wins.

Another reason why Englishwomen do not succeed as well as their neighbours over the water, is, it appears to me, that they are apt to despise the avocation by which they get their bread, and consequently not to put their hearts into it. A French milliner was asked to explain the reason of the superiority of her countrywomen in millinery. " They take pride in ther work," she replied, " and Englishwomen do not." A woman may think it a small thing to be employed all her life in making gowns, and may consider her occupation paltry and not worth thinking about more than is absolutely necessary to keep her situation, but she is wrong ; the *result* of the skill the French exercise in their work is not paltry, for they are well off compared to us, and the trade they bring to Paris greatly enriches their capital city, so they have a right to be proud. It is said that it requires five separate processes to make a pin, and that each process has a set of workmen attached to it who never do anything else. Now, it *does* sound as if making the fifth part of a pin all one's life was a petty avocation, but it is not a small *result* that England should make better pins than any other nation, and so supply the world. The pyramids are great things, yet each of the chisel-strokes and spadefuls of earth which went to make them was but a trifle. The means of effecting a purpose are often trivial, but we must not despise them, unless the *result* is trivial also. In all we undertake, however small the matter may be, it should ever be our aim to reach perfection. We ought not to be contented with passable workmanship, but should take a pride in our work and strive to make it the best possible.

Let us remember that every piece of good work done by a woman raises the character of the sex, and encourages employers to trust other women with more work of the same nature. We must also avoid discouragement, and ought never to allow ourselves to fancy, as many do, that because we are women we can do nothing well, and that therefore it is useless to try. We see that in France women can do many things which in England they never attempt; for, besides engaging in the various handicrafts already mentioned, they are continually employed as cashiers in shops, ticket clerks on railroads, and in various other public and private capacities, that are supposed in England to be quite beyond the intelligence of a woman. Our inferiority, therefore, is not natural and belonging to women as women, but is artificial, and confined to *untaught women*. It may be true that it would be difficult to find many women in England who could act as cashiers or railroad clerks, but the fact that Frenchwomen are constantly so employed proves that this incapability is not owing to sex, but to a bad education.

Now, this is very encouraging, for an artificial or accidental inferiority may be got rid of, and the effects of a bad education may with diligence be repaired by the young, and if the present generation do their duty, the next need not suffer from it at all. Perhaps our best plan to effect this object is, to observe in what the French system of education differs from ours, and to see whether we could not to some extent imitate it. In the first place, no person is allowed in France to set up a school, whether for boys or girls, or to take a situation as teacher, without passing an examination and receiving a certificate of competency ; thus good or at least tolerable teaching is secured ; and Mr. M. Arnold, who made a tour of inspection among schools in France, at the request of our Government, to observe their system, states that in girls' schools more attention is paid than with us to the practical parts of education, those parts I mean which will have a direct effect in enabling them to earn their bread. More than once he speaks of the great proficiency of the girls in arithmetic, and their corresponding deficiency in geography and history. It is impossible for children to study more than a certain number of hours, and in England we spend much time in teaching history and geography ; but the French, with greater shrewdness, reflect that these studies will have little effect in helping a girl to earn her bread, and consequently devote but little attention to them, reserving her time and energy for what will really be of use, namely, hand-writing and arithmetic. This explains the admission of women to offices in France for which they are considered incapable in England.

The superiority of Frenchwomen in dressmaking, and in some other arts, may be explained in the same manner. Girls at school are taught the cutting-out of dresses as well as how to sew; in fact, to teach a girl to sew without cutting-out, is teaching her but half her trade, and the worse-paid half, too; yet in England, we seldom, if ever, make the cutting-out of dresses a part of school teaching. To show the importance attached by the French to this practical instruction, it may be related that when the Empress lately visited the school at Paris for the daughters of members of the Legion of Honour, she instituted two prizes, one for the best painter on porcelain, the other for the best cutter-out of dresses.

In towns and large villages in France where there are several schools, they unite to establish an "ouvroir," or workroom, where, in the afternoon, when the literary schools are closed, the girls are taught needle-work in all its branches, including cutting-out, under the superintendence of an experienced and skilful workwoman, thus obviating the difficulty we suffer under in England, of finding a schoolmistress who can teach well both needle-work and the higher kinds of learning.*   In these

---

* For a short account of the "ouvroir" system, see "Popular Education in France," by Mathew Arnold, p. 104.

"ouvroirs," the special female industry of the district is also cultivated and brought to perfection; where embroidery on muslin is the special industry, good patterns are procured from the schools of design, which the children are taught to execute, thus at once exercising their skill, improving their taste, and diffusing good patterns among those who live by their industry. It is therefore not wonderful that the French surpass us in embroidery. I have seen it stated that lace-making is taught in the same way, and think it highly probable, but have not been able to find any account of it myself.

Now, when we consider what great advantages Frenchwomen enjoy by this good and useful instruction, we can no longer wonder at their superiority, nor need we tax our own countrywomen with natural inferiority of intelligence if they cannot equal them. But, whatever the causes of French superiority, one thing is certain—we must contrive to keep up with them in the race of ingenuity, skill, and energy, otherwise they will take our employments more and more away from us. Free trade is the order of the day, and whatever Frenchwomen make better than we do, is, and will be, brought over here duty free, and purchased in preference to our inferior wares. Millinery, lace, embroidery, and artificial flowers, are imported in quantities, and unless we can contrive to equal them, more and more will continue to be imported, to the great detriment of our own poor working women. It must be confessed that it is not a fair race, for their superior teaching gives them a terrible advantage; but still we must try to win, for we have no choice whether we will run in the race or not, and if we lose, we lose our daily bread.* Now, if to keep up with this competition is "head-work" on the part of our working women, it ought surely to be "heart-work" on the part of the wealthy, to aid them in the struggle by giving them good instruction and placing them as far as possible on an equal footing with their rivals.

In all plans for ameliorating the condition of women, it should be borne in mind that there are two distinct classes which want assistance, and that the assistance given to each requires to be of a very different character. There are the labouring classes, who want instruction in household and domestic matters, to enable them to

---

* It may, perhaps, seem ungenerous to grudge these poor French-women the profit their skill and industry makes out of English customers, a profit 'which by all accounts they want badly enough; but the fact is, that ill off as Frenchwomen are, our own countrywomen are in a still more deplorable condition. A study of the rate of wages given in "L'Ouvrière," beginning at page 205, will show this. Their most skilful female artificers in bronze, jewellery, and some other handicrafts, earn as much as 3s. 4d. a-day, and even more; thus, there is a large class of fairly-paid female artizans who have no counterpart in England, while the worse-paid kind of needlewomen do not certainly receive less than with us, and are perhaps a shade better remunerated. It is very remarkable that better wages should be earned by women in a country where there is so little outlet for the population by emigration. It is to be explained, I think, partly by the causes before adverted to, and partly by the liberality of French workmen, in allowing women to engage in trades from which they are excluded in England. Perhaps some day we may adopt the French system in these respects, and if we do, there can be little doubt that our women will then be better off than theirs, because of the greater advantages we possess as to emigration. Whenever this happens, it would be most ungenerous to grudge our neighbours any profit they can make out of us, but until then I confess that it seems to me impossible not to regret every sixpence which is withdrawn from our own countrywomen, and which they can so ill spare.

become good servants and useful wives for working men ; for these the teaching given in the "ouvroirs" would be of the highest value ; and there are the middle classes, such as the daughters of tradesmen, clerks, &c., who require another kind of teaching of a more intelléctual nature, to enable them to become saleswomen or book-keepers, and engage in other situations requiring intelligence ; for these a good business handwriting, a knowledge of arithmetic, mental and slate, and a thorough comprehension of book-keeping are desirable, and, above all, habits of diligence, obedience, and patient application. Bookkeeping is an excellent discipline for the mind, and ought invariably to be taught in schools for this class. It gives habits of neatness and order, and exercises the reason ; for if the pupils do not reflect, they are sure to make wrong entries. Children take interest in learning it, and it is certain to be of use in future life, whether the pupil remains single and has to support herself, or whether she marries and has to keep her household accounts. It is difficult to say which of these two classes of working women, the higher or the lower, most requires help. Each from want of instruc-tion and discipline, are apt to fall into great distress and misery, but all attempts at aid must be kept quite separate ; for tradesmen's daughters do not want to be taught to be servants, and it would be waste of time to give a high intellectual education to labourers' daughters, as such instruction would have no effect in aiding them to earn a living.

Yet, though different in detail, the principle to be observed in both classes of schools is the same, that of teaching things likely to be of practical use to the learners in after life. In both cases they should be made thoroughly to understand what they learn, as a girl's success in life depends upon being master of whatever she undertakes. A noble self-supporting ambition should be aroused, a truthful spirit encouraged, and obedience to lawful authority inculcated. A girl of the higher class requires to be taught self-command and the use and abuse of power; for as the future mistress of a household she will probably possess it, and those can never rule well who do not hold their own spirit in subjection. It is very important to impress high and honourable ideas on young girls, to implant self-respect, a love of justice, and to teach them to look with contempt on dishonest and deceitful conduct, and also, if possible to give them sound religious principles; for it is the women of a household who teach the rising generation, the religious and moral instruction of the children generally falling to the mother's lot.

To return to our subject, what working women can do to help themselves. First of all, they must try to excel in their branch of employment, whatever it is, and to do this they must be patient in learning their business. It is almost always disagreeable to learn, the process is tedious and wearisome, but success is unattainable without knowledge. The higher the description of work, the more difficult it is to learn. Manual work is soon learnt. It does not take more than a few weeks to train a cotton-spinner; but to attain to proficiency in any kind of intellectual work takes months, sometimes in the higher branches many years, of patient study and toil. Young

women and girls are often eager to learn at first, but
when they find that learning is a tedious process they
are discouraged, and give up. I have read a story about
the great and numerous nation of the Do-as-you-likes,
who came away from the country of Hard-work and set
up for themselves, but who were gradually reduced to
great misery and finally exterminated, because they never
would do anything that was disagreeable if they could
possibly avoid it. Many of the poor creatures in our
workhouses, prisons, and penitentiaries, belonged in their
time of prosperity to this great nation.

A spirit of endurance in encountering the many small
evils and discomforts which must be met with in earning
even a good livelihood is also quite necessary to all who
would succeed. A young artist was engaged to do some
work which could not be accomplished without considerable exposure to cold and fatigue. Her employer, seeing
that she looked tired and chilled, asked if she was not
suffering. "Yes," was the reply, given in a cheerful
tone, "yes, I am, but that is what I must expect."
This quiet answer had a touch of the heroic in it, quite
unsuspected by the speaker. She well knew that no one
could earn a living without encountering hardships, and
she had made up her mind to bear them cheerfully, as a
matter of course. This is the right spirit for workers.
Yet I would not advise young women to submit patiently
to hardships if they feel that their health is being
permanently injured. Health is the working-woman's
best dowry, without which she cannot earn her bread;
so, rather than lose it, even a well-paid situation should

be given up : it is only discomforts, petty annoyances,
and small hardships which should be disregarded.

There is, perhaps, no point on which employers are
more to blame than in exacting from their assistants such
long hours of toil as are likely to destroy the health of
ordinary women.   Even a poor maid-servant will be
grudged the eight hours' sleep which are absolutely
necessary to the health of all growing girls, and this will
be done by women who are not positively ill-disposed,
and will perhaps give money or old clothes to the poor,
and certainly contribute at church or chapel towards
charitable objects.   They forget that "to do justly" is
the first duty of life ; and that if everyone was *just*,
there would be little occasion for anyone to be *generous.*
The poor girl thus over-worked will one day break down
and become an object for charitable relief ; but had her
mistress acted justly towards her, she would have continued able to earn her living for herself.   It is the same
with milliners' and dressmakers' assistants and apprentices.   They are often kept far too long at work, and
early death, or long pining illness, which to a working
girl is worse than death, are the consequences.   Perhaps,
some who read these pages may themselves become
employers.   I trust that they will think seriously of their
responsibility : they could not better prepare themselves
for it than by reading the Epistle of St. James ; and
every year it would be well to keep the anniversary of
their accession to power by reading it carefully over
again.   We hear of co-operative associations being successful in many trades : why should they not succeed
among dressmakers ?   Then, the same persons being

capitalists and workers, the receivers of wages and the payers of wages, justice would certainly be observed.

A few words on the subject of obedience to lawful authority will perhaps not be out of place here. Discipline is necessary in all undertakings. What a scene of confusion would an army be without it! And the same is true of smaller concerns. Whether the chief be the employer, or, as in co-operative associations, an elected officer, obedience is still necessary. An associate, assistant, or servant, has no right to quarrel with terms to which she has voluntarily agreed. If she does not like them she may seek a better situation, but she has no right to complain unless deception has been practised upon her.

Far be it from me, however, to say that submission is invariably a duty. There are cases when submission but invites oppression, and resistance becomes a necessity. The person who resists generally loses by it, but others are benefited and protected. It may also, when the interests of others are concerned, sometimes become our duty to submit, when if no one but ourself was concerned we should resist. In either case, those who submit and those who resist contrary to their own advantage for the sake of others, act nobly, and show a generous spirit. But, though submission is not invariably a duty, the necessity for resistance should be considered an evil, not a pleasure, as is done by some pugnacious spirits, nor should it be resorted to unless an equitable arrangement can be concluded in no other way. Neither should it be embarked in for trifling causes, or without a strong probability of success, for a quelled insurrection does but rivet the slave's chain the tighter. Also, it is a duty to avoid fancying ourselves the victims of oppression when we really are not; injustice is not such a small sin that we can afford to accuse each other of it lightly. Nothing wears into the soul so much as the belief that we are unfairly dealt with, therefore it is not wise to foster the thought unnecessarily. "A merry heart goes all the day, a sad one tires in a mile—a," says the old song, and for this reason, though not for this reason only, a sensitive spirit should be discouraged. People sometimes admire a sensitive spirit in themselves, but let me ask, did they ever admire it in others? A sensitive mind, like a delicate constitution or weak nerves, is a source of failure, not a subject for pride.

Gentleness is a virtue which deserves much consideration. If I were to write a table of the qualities which most conduce towards success, I should put gentleness very high in the list, next, perhaps, to energy and perseverance. A request gently proffered is far more likely to be granted, than a demand, however just, if it be roughly enforced: it is useful, too, when it is necessary to refuse. It was said of a great politician that he could refuse a request in such a gentle, kind way that he almost seemed to confer a favour; while of some other statesman it was said that he granted a favour so roughly as to offend the person on whom it was conferred. Thus, gentleness makes friends and saves us from making enemies. It is as easy to say, "I am sorry I cannot comply with your wishes," as "I will do no such thing, and I wonder you should ask me;" but how different is the effect produced on the hearer! Gentleness is quite compatible with firmness—indeed is one of its adjuncts ; for people often refuse an unreasonable request so harshly that they grant it afterwards to make up for their incivility. Even in a quarrel a gentle manner and as far as possible gentle words should be maintained. Cutting speeches and sharp taunts are of no use, and only serve to make a settlement of the point in dispute more difficult. We should remember that success in life depends as much on our moral as on our intellectual qualities. A gentle, good-tempered woman of average abilities will succeed as well, in all probability, as a clever woman with rough manners and a sharp tongue : of course a woman who is both clever and good-tempered will succeed better than either.

Good manners are important in every profession and business, and in some are absolutely necessary. A writer in *Macmillan's Magazine* says, " Manner is the one and indispensable essential in a linendrapers' assistant. Without this virtue all others vanish into thin air ; they are lost in the shade and go for nothing." This is equally true of every kind of salesman or saleswoman, and the higher the class of shop, the more obliging and polished the manners of the assistants are expected to be. Persons of a naturally obliging disposition will have less trouble in attaining to good manners than others, and persons of a mild nature can more easily learn to be gentle in word or deed ; still, good manners and gentleness are probably unattainable to few. It is a great blessing to be possessed of both a good heart and a good head, but where one is deficient, the other should be called upon to do double work to

K

compensate for the shortcomings of its comrade. Thus, when gentleness does not arise from natural good-feeling, it should be produced by reflection ; and, *per contra*, the wisdom which the intellect fails to supply must be obtained by steady, heartfelt adherence to the rules of right and wrong, which, in nine cases out of ten, indicate precisely the same course that the most consummate worldly wisdom would point out.   There are probably few middle-aged people who in looking back on their lives, do not perceive that they have committed some foolish action, from which they would have been preserved had they done simply what was right.   The wisdom of the heart in humbly obeying the directions God in His kindness has given to guide us, would often and often make up for the folly of the head.   The saying that '' Honesty is good policy,'' is equally true of every virtue under the sun.   It is always bad policy in the long run to do wrong, though we may gain by it at the moment.   If we were perfectly wise we should see this, but as we are not wise, we fail to see it, and do wrong, and do not discover till long afterwards that if we had done right it would have been more to our advantage.

Now, to conclude, I will say a few words on public spirit, for it is a quality in which women are often deficient, and this is a cause for regret, as it has more power than any other in checking selfishness.   Women are seldom selfish in their own families, often are they most nobly generous, sometimes even foolishly so ; but towards those for whom they have no affection, women are often selfish.   Their unselfishness to their relations is the result of love, not of principle.   Thus, the same woman will sometimes be kind and generous to her friends and relatives, yet a hard and grasping mistress to her dependants, and unfair in her dealings with her equals.

I believe that associations, such as benefit clubs and co-operation societies, would have a strong effect in producing public spirit, calling out a love of justice, and teaching women to rejoice in the general prosperity of a number of associates and friends, instead of rejoicing each in her own prosperity alone or that of her family, and thinking of no one else. It is true that each person must think first and most of his or her own concerns, but to think *first* and *most* is not to think *solely* of them. When we reflect how many interests in common women have, it is sad to see how little union there is among them. It is this want of union which makes women so weak and defenceless. Like the sticks in the fable, they are easily broken one by one, instead of being closely bound together by the ties of sisterly love and mutual sympathy. Good and great men are trying to raise the position of women, but these efforts will be unavailing unless zealously seconded by the women themselves. Every woman who has her own livelihood to earn, whatever her station may be, has suffered more or less either from a deficient education, or from ill-judged restrictions excluding her from well-remunerated employments ; even those who are successful suffered from these causes early in their career. Truly, these mutual misfortunes, this common suffering, ought to form a strong bond of union among all who work for their bread, whether they belong to the higher or lower sections of society. Indeed, it

seems as if so hard a case ought to secure the sympathy
and aid of every woman, whether she belongs to the
ranks of those who work or not.*

There are two descriptions of workers who specially
deserve the support of their own sex. First, good
teachers, who, by the instruction they give, raise the
intelligence of their pupils and make them useful,
helpful members of society; and secondly, women of
enterprise, who leave the beaten track of labour, and
seek out fresh paths for themselves. It has been said
that the man who makes an ear of corn grow where none
grew before is a benefactor to his race: the same may
be said of the woman who opens a new employment to
her sex. The generous worker who, to avoid distressing
others, declines to enter on an overcrowded employment
and strikes out in a new line, will have to encounter
many difficulties; but of one support and consolation she
ought always to feel secure—the gratitude and respect of
her fellow-women.

It is probable that in time women will be better
educated, and gradually assume their proper industrial
position. Yet, though these changes may take place *in*
the course of time, they will not take place *by* the course
of time, but only by means of efforts which in the course
of time may prove successful: if there are no efforts

* Professor Wilson, when anxious to establish an industrial museum,
appealed for assistance specially to intelligent ladies, on the ground that
they would thereby contribute "to increase the means of giving an
industrial education to women of the poorer classes, and to multiply the
vocations which may keep them from starvation, misery, and crime.—
"Memoirs of Geo. Wilson," p. 425.

there will be no improvement. Meanwhile, I would say
to the workers for their bread, in the words of Dr. John
Brown, "My young friends, mix brains with everything
and everything with brains." Remember that every step
in advance is gain, every increase in skill, in taste, in the
knowledge of art, in general intelligence, power of
reasoning, and accurate calculation, is so much towards a better state of things, so much towards raising
the condition of our country-women and the depressed
state of our female industry. And this is far from
a small object: the means by which it is to effected may
appear trivial, but the result cannot be despised. Each
step in advance may seem short; each stroke with the
pencil or the pen, each stitch with the needle, may have
little effect; each simple piece of practical knowledge
acquired, each effort of reasoning successfully made,
may seem but little gained; but added together they
come to a good deal. The ants in tropical countries
build houses twelve feet high, yet each ant brings but a
grain of dust at a time. To raise the condition of our
female industry is an object to which women of every degree
may contribute according to the talents entrusted to
them, the rich aiding in their way, the poor in theirs;
but success most depends on the exertions of the poor,
for the rich can only give them the means of instruction
and self-help: it rests with the workers to avail themselves of these means. If every worker would put heart
and head into her work and do her best, whether with
pen, or brush, or ledger, or needle, whatever her tool
may be—not only for the purpose of earning her own
bread, but for the noble object of raising the position of

her fellow-women—the condition of workers generally
would before long improve. This is a purpose worthy to
occupy both our heads and hearts, and the humblest
worker in the cause, if she does her best, deserves
respect. Let it, then, be our object in all we do to help,
not only ourselves but each other, and let us strive so to
live and work, as to show that self-help is far removed
from selfishness.*

* I wish to correct a mistake in the Chapter on "Choice of a
Business." I have spoken of the Female Medical College as if the
students there could obtain diplomas or licenses as general medical
practitioners. This is not the case; they can only obtain certificates for
midwifery.   The instruction given on the subject is said to be good, and
this branch offers a fair opening for remunerative employment to women
of some education; but the ladies instructed there are not enabled to
engage legally in any other part of the profession. It is, however,
possible for women to enter the general medical profession, and the
Secretary of the Society for the Employment of Women, can place ladies
wishing to enter it in communication with a lady who has obtained a
license to act as general practitioner, and who will give information upon
the course necessary to be pursued.

APPENDIX.

A.

Female School of Art, and House Decorators.

Instruction in decorations of all kinds is given at the Female School of Art, 43, Queen Square, Bloomsbury, by Dr. Dresser, F.L.S. Terms, £5 for a session of 20 weeks. Students and free scholars of the School of Art, are admitted for £2. Orders for house decorations and designs of all kinds are received at the School.

Wood engraving is also taught, as well as all styles of drawing and painting. Applications to be made to the lady superintendent, Miss Gann.

B.

Institutions for Training Nurses.

The committee of the Nightingale Fund train nurses at St. Thomas's Hospital, age from 25 to 35. The training lasts a year. Probationers are kept, free of expense, and receive a small salary; at the end of a year situations in hospitals are found them. Applications to be made to Mrs. Wardroper, Matron, St. Thomas's Hospital, London, S.E.

St. John's House Training Institution. *Norfolk Street, Strand, London.*

Age between 25 and 40. Period of probation according to capacity. Probationers and nurses kept free. Wages,

first year £10 : gradually rising to £20 ; 5s. a month extra
during actual attendance on the sick. A superannuation
fund is being formed. Applications to be made to the Lady
Superintendent.

ALL SAINTS' HOME. 82, *Margaret Street, Cavendish
Square, London.*

Women of a superior class, as well as those of humble
degree, are received here. Age of probationers from 20 to
45. Time of training three months ; board, lodging, and
washing found. Nurses are paid besides on the following
scale :

	£	s.	d.
1st year	10	10	0
2nd „	12	0	0
3rd „	14	0	0
4th „	16	0	0
5th „	18	0	0

After the fifth year a nurse will receive £20 without
further increase.

Each nurse will have *two print dresses and two best
dresses* given her every year ; must belong to the Church
of England, be of good character, and able to read and
write. Application to be made to the Mother Superior, at
the Home, from whom further particulars can be ascertained.

INSTITUTION OF NURSING SISTERS. 4, *Devonshire Square,
Bishopsgate, London, N.E.*

Age of probationers from 28 to 40 ; must be intelligent
and of good character. Time of probation, several weeks,
when, if found qualified, they are received as sisters.
Stipend, first year, £20 ; third, £23 ; fifth, £25 ; board,
lodging, dress, &c. After twelve years' service a superannuation pension of £20 per annum Candidates to apply
personally to the Lady Superintendent at the Institution,
between 9 and 12. This Institution was founded by
Mrs. Fry.

LIVERPOOL TRAINING SCHOOL AND HOME FOR NURSES.

Age of probationers from 25 to 35, certificates of age, health, and character required. Wages of probationers after the first three months, £14 4s. a year, with board, lodging, and washing. At the end of the year they become nurses, when they will be required to serve two more years in hospital, or as they may be directed, after which time they are free to engage in private nursing. Application to be made to the Lady Superintendent of the Training School for Nurses, Royal Infirmary, Liverpool.

BATH TRAINING INSTITUTION AND HOME FOR NURSES.

Age from 20 to 35 years. Qualifications—good health and character, able to read and write. A premium of three guineas is required with each candidate, and an agreement is entered into after a month's trial, to serve the Institution for three years. Wages, £8 a year to probationers, £12 to nurses. After three years the nurses are at liberty to engage in private nursing, or to remain in the Institution at higher wages. Application to be made to the Lady Superintendent, 7, Duke Street, Bath. Arrangements are being made to receive educated women (ladies in reduced circumstances) and instruct them in midwifery and monthly nursing.

BRISTOL TRAINING INSTITUTION.

The system is almost the same as at Bath, wages rather higher. Apply to the Hon. Secretary, 5, Cambridge Place, Clifton, Bristol.

Women are also trained as nurses in almost every hospital; for though ready-trained nurses are preferred, it is almost impossible to obtain a sufficient number. The best treatment is given in the Government Army Hospitals.

ARMY HOSPITALS.

Age of nurses from 30 to 40; must be able to write and produce a certificate of good character. Wages commence at £20 a year, with board, lodging, and uniform dress, and are raised at the rate of £2 a year till they reach £50. At 60 every nurse must retire on a pension. Pension after ten years' service, £12 a year; an addition of rather more than a pound is made for each subsequent year's service, until £35 is reached.

Eight hours·are allowed for sleep, two for recreation, besides time for meals. If a nurse loses her health before she has served ten years, she receives a small gratuity to enable her to rest while recovering. A woman of good education is almost certain to rise in a few months to some superior office.

Nurses trained under the Nightingale fund at St. Thomas' Hospital, are often sent to Military Hospitals; but application may also be made to the Superintendent General of nurses, Royal Victoria Hospital, Netley, Southampton.

———

At the following Institutions in London, women can be trained as midwives:—

QUEEN CHARLOTTE'S LYING-IN HOSPITAL. *New Road, Marylebone, N.W.*

Two classes of pupils are admitted. The first class have a bedroom and sitting-room to themselves, are comfortably boarded, and received instruction from the medical officers. Fee, £30 for three months' training. The second class sleep and live in common, cook their own meals, and receive no instruction from the medical officers, but are taught by the matron and nurses. Fee, £8 8s. for three months. Applications to be made to the Secretary or Matron at the Hospital.

BRITISH LYING-IN HOSPITAL. *Endell Street, Long Acre, W.C.*

Resident pupils admitted. Applications to be made to the Secretary, from whom further particulars can be ascertained.

KING'S COLLEGE HOSPITAL, *Portugal Street, London, W.C.*

Respectable women between 26 and 34 years of age are here taught midwifery. The period of training is six months, instruction is given gratis, but £10 must be paid in advance for board, lodging, and washing. A certificate of good health and references as to character will be required. Probationers are received on the 31st of October and 30th April in each year. Applications should be made not less than a fortnight previously, to the Lady Superintendent, from whom a printed paper of regulations can be obtained.

CITY OF LONDON HOSPITAL, *City Road, E.C.*

GENERAL LYING-IN HOSPITAL, *York Road, Lambeth.*

ROYAL MATERNITY CHARITY, Office, 2, *Chatham Place, Blackfriars, E.C.* 35 midwives employed.

ROYAL PIMLICO LYING-IN INSTITUTION, 38, *Upper Belgrave Place, Pimlico, S.W.*

ST. GEORGE'S AND ST. JAMES' LYING-IN CHARITY, 17, *Savile Row, W.*

At these places instruction can be obtained on various terms, the particulars of which had better be ascertained from the resident officers. I fear that the course of instruction seldom, if ever, exceeds three months, a term insufficient to enable a pupil to attain to much skill; but probably the pupil might often obtain an engagement as midwife after the term was over, and thus have the opportunity of practising under experienced medical men before setting up for herself. Educated women should study the subject before going, that they may derive as much benefit as possible from the instruction afforded.

At the Female Medical College, 4, Fitzroy Square, W.C., lectures are given on Midwifery. A course of study at this College would be an excellent preparation for the practical instruction obtained at the Lying-in Institutions.

C.

OFFICE IN LONDON WHERE LAW COPYING CAN BE LEARNT :—

12, *Portugal Street, Lincoln's Inn, W.C.*

Fee, £1. Six months are required to learn the business really well as a clerk, but pupils can begin to earn money much sooner. MSS. are copied, circulars written, and every kind of writing executed at the same place. Two years' instruction would be required for the head of an establishment.

D.

COMMERCIAL SCHOOL FOR GIRLS, 45, *Great Ormond Street, W.C.*

Terms, 9d. a week for children above ten, 6d. for those under ten.

Classes for training young women as clerks and book-keepers are held at the Working Woman's College, 29, Queen's Square, W.C. Fee, 5s. for a term of 14 or 15 weeks.

E.

COOKING SCHOOLS.

16, *Soho Square.* Director, Mrs. Langton. A Register Office is kept here. The terms of instruction can be had on application. 281, *Regent Street.* Director, Mrs. Mitchell.

F.

EMIGRATION OFFICES.

Government Office for Domestic Servants, 3, Park Street, Westminster. Free passages.

National Female Emigration Society. Office for Domestic Servants, 44, Charing Cross.
Assisted passages to Australia, New Zealand, and the Colonies.

COLONIAL EMIGRATION.

Commissioner for Canada. Office, Dray's Buildings, Water Street, Liverpool.

Commissioner for Queensland. Office, 17, Gracechurch Street, London.

Commissioners for Canterbury. Office, 16, Charing Cross.

Commissioners for Adelaide. Office, 5, Copthall Court, Throgmorton Street, E.C.

Commissioner for Otago. Office, 36, Leadenhall Street, E.C., and 20, St. Andrew Square, Edinburgh.

Any kind of women of good character taken.

Commissioner for Southland. Office, 3, Adelaide Place, King William Street, E.C. Assisted passages.

MIDDLE CLASS FEMALE EMIGRATION SOCIETY, 12, *Portugal Street, Lincoln's Inn, W.C.*

Assisted passages to all the Colonies given to nursery governesses and practically-educated women. Secretaries, Miss Rye and Miss Jane Lewin.

G.

HOMES FOR YOUNG WOMEN IN LONDON.

As young women in business, or coming to town to learn a trade, or to seek employment, or prepare for emigration, are often at a loss to find cheap yet comfortable and respectable lodgings, the following Homes have been established to receive them; but I strongly recommend no one to come to London to seek employment, as it is more difficult to be procured there than in the country.

CHRISTIAN YOUNG WOMEN'S HOME, 50, *Charlotte Street, Fitzroy Square, W.C.*

Terms 10s. a week for board and lodging; 12s. with a private bedroom.

CHRISTIAN YOUNG WOMEN'S HOME, 48, *Crawford Street, Portman Square.*

Terms 5s. a week.

In all cases lodging alone is given when required, or partial board on reduced terms.

H.

NEEDLEWOMEN'S INSTITUTION,

Where ladies can engage workwomen at 1s. 6d. a day.

2, *Hinde Street, Manchester Square.*   Secretary, Miss Barlee.

Any additional useful information will be gratefully received by the Author, at the office of the Society for the Employment of Women, 19, Langham Place.

JARROLD AND SONS, PRINTERS, NORWICH.

For EU product safety concerns, contact us at Calle de José Abascal, 56–1°, 28003 Madrid, Spain or eugpsr@cambridge.org.